Praise for *Julian of Norwich: Wisdom in a Time of Pandemic—and Beyond*

Suppose you had a wise woman friend who was a scholar—and also the survivor of a plague many times longer and more lethal than the one we are going through now. Wouldn't you want to know what she has to say? Thanks to Matthew Fox, we can find a friend in *Julian of Norwich*, exactly the mental, emotional, and spiritual vaccine we need now.

—Gloria Steinem

I think of Matthew Fox as "God's Talent Scout" for all the pivotal figures and ideas he has reclaimed for the reform of Christianity. He knows the sources and translates them into modern idiom for the rest of us! What he has done with Hildegard, Eckhart, and Aquinas himself makes him a major teacher and guide. Now in our parallel time of pandemic, he does it again with Lady Julian of Norwich—as we all ask "What does it mean to love and believe now?"

—Richard Rohr, OFM, Center for Action and Contemplation, Albuquerque, New Mexico

If ever there was a time when the presence and the power of a book and the felt need of the moment came together this is surely it. Matthew Fox's "Julian" is the answer to the spiritual and emotional meaning of a pandemic. It turns both the frustration and the fear of Covid-19 into a period of new insight into the spiritual life. It gives us all new understanding of what we must each do to grow in peace and joy and life not only despite this pandemic but because of it.

Most of all, this book is highly enjoyable to read, totally accessible whatever a person's experience with the period of the Bubonic Plague. Do I recommend this book? Totally. Give yourself a gift of new spiritual energy.

—Sr. Joan Chittister, OSB

Warrior brother to the Feminine, Rev. Father Mathew Fox, like a tender archaeologist brushes away the sands of time under which lay the remarkable blessings and cogent views of Julian who wrote in the time of plague, so very similar to our times. This work is its own kind of spiritual vaccine to help keep one's head even if some others are losing theirs. In this, as always, Matthew Fox anoints modern Souls with a medicine he finds in the old and venerable Holy voices.

—Dr Clarissa Pinkola Estés Reyés Poet,
Traditional Medicine practitioner,
Post-trauma Recovery Specialist, Psychoanalyst, author of
Women Who Run with the Wolves and
Untie The Strong Woman on La Señora de Guadalupe

What an utterly magnificent book. The work of Julian of Norwich, lovingly supported by the genius of Matthew Fox, is a roadmap into the heart of the eco-spiritual truth that all life breathes together. All of Julian's teachings are an expression of the profound truth that All is One with God and Nature. If ever a book was written for this time of pandemic chaos and transformation, it is this one.

—Caroline Myss, author of *Intimate Conversations with the Divine: Prayer, Guidance, and Grace*

Matthew Fox, in this gorgeous, brilliant, and beautifully written book, invites us into the heart of one of the greatest Christian mystics, Julian of Norwich. He shows us that Julian is an extraordinarily intense and inspiring guide for our time. She herself lived in a time of plague and social cataclysm, but never lost her hope in humanity or her joy in the divine presence. This inspired book will attune you to timeless truths in the middle of a whirlwind of distress and chaos and will inspire in you the courage to go on deepening your relationship with God and standing up for the glory of the creation. I cannot recommend it highly enough.

—Andrew Harvey, author of *The Hope* and *Radical Regeneration*

What a book of consolation! Matthew Fox once again brings to the reader Julian's mystical insights into the oneness of all. Julian lived during a global pandemic and saw through the fear and grief to the nearness of the divine. I found this both comfort and challenge. During our time of social distancing, may we break with the historical culture of power and domination to recover Julian's awareness of the divine vibrant in love and compassion at the core of all of creation.

—Sr. Simone Campbell, SSS, Executive Director,
"http://www.networklobby.org/" NETWORK Lobby for
Catholic Social Justice, author of *Hunger for Hope.*

I believe that Julian of Norwich is a mystic-prophet for our time who offers us a quiet but profound revolution in consciousness... states author Matthew Fox. In **Julian of Norwich: Wisdom in a Time of Pandemic--and Beyond,** Fox introduces us to a highly educated, visionary woman who lived as an anchorite and wrote during the Bubonic Plague. Fox's years of writing and teaching Creation Centered Spirituality and the Wisdom Tradition opens our eyes to Julian's Feminine aspect of God, goodness and to her wisdom urgently needed during this time of revolution, pandemic, and climate change.

—The Reverend Dr. Lauren Artress, author of
*Walking a Sacred Path: Rediscovering the
Labyrinth as a Spiritual Practice*

A marvelous introduction to the visionary yet grounded world of Julian of Norwich, one of the greatest spiritual writers of the Middle Ages. Her messages about God in nature and the divine feminine are more relevant today than ever. Matthew Fox makes her insights freshly accessible and inspiringly relates her work both to her spiritual ancestors and also to our current crises.

—Rupert Sheldrake, PhD, biologist and author
of *Science and Spiritual Practices*

It is a privilege and an honor to be able to call Matthew a friend for 30 years now. As an author myself, his prolificness never fails to impress and awe me. I believe that one day he will be included in the pantheon of mystics he so beautifully honors and keeps alive for us. This latest book on Julian of Norwich is presciently timely for these challenging times of plagues, fear, and uncertainty. Thank you, Matt, for your commitment, your courage, your teachings—for all you do on all our behalf!

—Christian de la Huerta, Author of *Awakening the Soul of Power*

Julian *of* Norwich:
Wisdom in a Time of Pandemic—*and* Beyond

Matthew Fox

JULIAN OF NORWICH: WISDOM IN A TIME OF PANDEMIC—AND BEYOND

iUniverse books may be ordered through booksellers or by contacting:

iUniverse
1663 Liberty Drive
Bloomington, IN 47403
www.iuniverse.com
844-349-9409

ISBN: 978-1-6632-0868-2 (sc)
ISBN: 978-1-6632-0869-9 (e)

This book is available in e-book form. It is available in audio format from http://www.matthewfox.org.

Print information available on the last page.

iUniverse rev. date: 04/30/2021

I dedicate this book to women everywhere (and the men who love them) who are being asked to speak their truth in words and actions in defense of Mother Earth and all her creatures. In this time of excessive patriarchy, may wisdom prevail over folly, love over fear, compassion over hate, justice over injustice, the mammal brain over the reptilian brain so that future generations may thrive. All in the spirit of our sister Julian, who insisted that "we are born into a birthright of never-ending joy."

"Wisdom is the mother of all good things."
                                    —Wisdom 7:11-12

The first good thing is the goodness of nature.
God is the same thing as nature.
The goodness in nature is God.
God feels great delight to be our Father.
God feels great delight to be our Mother.
We experience a wondrous mix of well and woe.
The mingling of both well and distress in us
        is so astonishing
        that we can hardly tell which state
        we or our neighbor are in—
        that's how astonishing it is!
                —Julian of Norwich

CONTENTS

FOREWORD

MIRABAI STARR

"All will be well," says the medieval English mystic we call Julian of Norwich. "And all will be well," she says again. Then, in case we didn't take that in the first two times, she repeats with lucid zest, "and *every kind of thing* shall be well."

In a time of global pandemic and rampant racial injustice, this may sound like a spiritual bypass (borrowing an apt term from contemporary Buddhist psychology to convey the impulse to check out of painful experiences by means of religious platitudes and practices). But it's quite the opposite. Julian, who lived through many rounds of the Black Death, experienced unspeakable suffering within and around her. If, as historic records indicate, up to 50 percent of the population of Europe died during the plague, then, statistically speaking, Julian may have lost half of the people she was closest to. For those of us whose lives have been marked by multiple deaths of loved ones, such a notion is difficult to absorb. How can anyone bear such sorrow and survive?

We cannot.

Who we thought we were dies when a beloved dies. And it takes a while for a new self to rise, often haltingly, from the ashes of our ravaged hearts. But when we turn toward the fire of grief rather than run from it, we are transformed. Stripped of extraneous concerns and outmoded values, we often find ourselves abiding in liminal space and discover it to be sacred ground. It is from such a naked place that Julian experienced her sixteen "revelations of divine love" in which Christ, who reveals himself to be God-the-Mother, convinces Julian that sin and damnation are human constructs and that there is not an iota of wrath in God. In fact, He/She assures the fledgling mystic, our mistakes and our wounds make us all the more adorable to this unconditionally loving God of ours.

Sound familiar?

When Fr. Matthew Fox's groundbreaking book *Original Blessing* was published in 1983, it revolutionized the Christian community by daring to suggest that (as Christ told Julian in her visons) we replace our preoccupation with original sin with an openness to wonder, recognizing that every particle of creation is imbued with goodness. Including you— and me. And every other being, human and otherwise. Fox was rewarded for his theological generosity with being formally silenced by the Catholic Church for fourteen months. A few years later, he was expelled from the Dominican Order to which he had belonged for over three decades. While painful, this break with his beloved tradition catapulted him into the center of his prophetic calling, in turn gifting the world with the treasure of creation spirituality. This book of reflections on the teachings of Julian of Norwich and their startling relevance for our times is, in many respects, the ripened fruit of Fox's decades of cultivating a spirituality of radical blessedness.

Julian's visions of the passion of Christ arose from the depths of her own suffering and bequeathed the rest of us the most extravagantly optimistic theology of the Christian landscape. At the age of thirty, stricken by a grave illness and believing she was on her deathbed, Julian let go. At least, she tried. She hints that at this time she had nothing to live for and so she welcomed death. On the threshold between this world and the next, Julian encountered the living Christ not as a remote and tortured sacrificial victim but rather as "friendly" and "merry," as warm and welcoming.

In her "showings," as she called them, Christ revealed his bleeding and his dying as acts of unconditional love. "The blood of Christ nourishes and feeds all living things," my friend, iconographer priest William Hart McNichols told me during a recent conversation about Julian of Norwich, "just like our earthly mothers feed and sustain us in the womb." Who but a mother, Julian asks, would break herself open and pour herself out for love of her children? Redemption, then, is not a matter of absolving sin; it is about loving us into the wholeness of who we really are.

The first woman to write in English, Julian recorded her showings immediately following her near-death experience. This is known as the "short text." Then she walled herself into an anchor hold and spent the rest of her life contemplating the meaning of these visions and offering her unfolding wisdom in the form of the "long text." Her choice to live as an anchoress arose from a desire to focus on the extraordinary gifts she had been given in her intimate exchange with Christ-the-Mother. And it was a way to quarantine during a time when infectious disease was rending the fabric of society and people lived in a collective state of fear and uncertainty.

As we grapple with the ravages of COVID-19, we, too, are invited to turn inward. This enforced enclosure is an opportunity to reimagine a world we would like to live in and leave to our children, a reality permeated by values of loving-kindness and fearless truth-telling, of voluntary simplicity and care for the stranger, of taking our rightful place in the web of interbeing and welcoming all of creation as family.

It is worth pointing out that Julian of Norwich was not a hermit. Even as she spent more than forty years living in a small cell attached to a church, she had a window that looked out onto the busy city street of Norwich. From this window she offered spiritual guidance to her community. She kept tabs on neighborhood news and soothed broken hearts. She accepted loaves of fresh baked bread and shared honey from the hives she kept. She was simultaneously protected from the world and connected to the earth.

I am grateful to the wise and joyous voice of Matthew Fox, who helps mystics like Julian of Norwich—and her sister mystic, Hildegard of Bingen—sing across the centuries and transfigure our hearts now, when we need them most.

INTRODUCTION

JULIAN'S TIME OF
PANDEMIC AND OURS

A time of crisis and chaos, the kind that a pandemic brings, is, among other things, a time to call on our ancestors for their deep wisdom. Not just knowledge but true *wisdom* is needed in a time of death and profound change, for at such times we are beckoned not simply to return to the immediate past, that which we remember fondly as "the normal," but to reimagine a new future, a renewed humanity, a more just and therefore sustainable culture, and one even filled with joy.

Julian of Norwich (1342–ca.1415) is one of those ancestors calling to us today. After all, she lived her entire life during a raging pandemic. Julian is a stunning thinker, a profound theologian and mystic, a fully awake woman, and a remarkable guide with a mighty vision to share for twenty-first-century seekers. She is a special chaperone for those navigating a time of pandemic. Julian knew a thing or two about "sheltering in place," because she was an anchoress—that is, someone who, by definition, is literally walled up inside a small space for life. Julian also knew something about fostering a spirituality that can survive the trauma of a pandemic. While others all about her were freaking out about nature gone awry, Julian kept her spiritual and intellectual composure, staying grounded and true to her belief in the goodness of life, creation, and humanity and, in no uncertain terms, inviting others to do the same.

What an amazing gift we have from Julian—a profound treatise written in three movements over several decades from within the bowels of one of the worsts pandemics in human history. Surely she has deep lessons to share with us today.

Life in a Pandemic

In Julian's day, Norwich was the second largest and richest city in England; only London was larger and more affluent. The cathedral was a Benedictine priory of great prestige and opulence, not unlike the monastery-cathedrals of Canterbury and Durham, and the Norwich library was considered "one of the finest in late medieval England."[1]

The plague first struck in Norwich in 1349, when Julian was only seven years old, but it kept returning in waves. The plague returned from 1361 to 1364, in 1368 and 1371, from 1373 (the year Julian received her visions and wrote her first book) to 1375, in 1390, and again in 1405 and on into the fifteenth century. By the 1370's, when Julian wrote her first book, the population of England was cut in half. So many people died that they were buried five deep in mass graves. All the street cleaners in London died of the plague, and two out of three clergy died—and probably the best and bravest since they were serving the sick and dying when they caught the deadly disease.

The bubonic plague was terrifying and ugly. One's body would become riddled with ugly sores and scars, and black boils would ooze blood and pus. Upon contracting the disease, at least in the earlier outbreaks, one would typically be dead in three to four days. It was so contagious that touching infected clothes could be deadly. One could go to bed healthy at night and be dead by the morning. It traveled through the air as well as on fleas and rats. I call it AIDS on steroids. And not only was it was highly contagious, but there was no Center for Disease Control or World Health Organization to inform populations of the source or how to avoid it, and certainly no hopes or promises of a vaccine.

Historians now believe it killed between one in two and one in three persons in Europe. Like COVID-19, however, it was a *global* disease—it spread through China, India, Persia, Syria, and Egypt before it came to Europe via sailing vessels. One way to combat it was to force sailors to stay on ships for forty days after anchoring, only allowing them to come ashore if they were well after forty days—thus the term *quarantine* (from the word for forty).

Yes, this was the pandemic that stared Julian in the face her whole life long. She must have grown up with death and fear all around her. Yet she did not flinch.

Creation Spirituality and the Showings

Julian's visions or "showings" occurred in 1373, when she was thirty years of age. She wrote what is known as her "short" book shortly after. Decades later, with deeper and deeper reflection and unpacking of the messages she received, she wrote a longer version of her visions in what was in effect two editions. Thus, she edited and re-edited her book through her lifetime.

Julian's response to the pandemic, as we know it from her two books, are amazingly grounded in a love of life and gratitude. Instead of running from death, she actually prayed to enter into it and it is from that experience of death all around her and meditating on the cruel crucifixion of Christ that she interpreted as a communal, not just a personal event, that her visions arrived.

Mirabai Starr calls hers a "radically optimistic theology"—this in a time of pandemic no less![2] What is remarkable about her life and teaching is that instead of yielding to despair or blame, she sought out in depth the goodness of life and creation. Indeed, she established her entire worldview on this sense of goodness and the sacred marriage of grace and nature, a sense of God-in-nature or *panentheism*.

Julian was a champion of the divine feminine in a century when patriarchy ruled. Starr writes that she "reveals the feminine side of God" and "gently and lovingly defies the patriarchy at almost every turn."[3] Julian insisted that the feminine penetrate every aspect of our understanding of the divine, all dimensions of a triune God. She is a forceful spokesperson for the "motherhood of God" in our day when matricide, the killing of girls and women, wisdom, creativity and compassion, a matricide that culminates in the despoiling and crucifixion of Mother Earth, is going on everywhere.

Julian was a stalwart student, practitioner, and teacher of the creation spirituality tradition, one rooted in the same wisdom tradition of the Bible in which the historical Jesus stood. It is also found richly in St. Benedict and his sister Scholastica, as well as in Hildegard of Bingen, the renaissance woman and Benedictine abbess who composed many songs and an opera, offered healing remedies to many, wrote ten books, painted mandalas of her visions, and challenged both emperors and popes from her abbey in twelfth-century Germany. Creation spirituality forms the matrix of Celtic spirituality and was foundational to Francis of Assisi, Thomas Aquinas, Mechtild of Magdeburg and Meister Eckhart, all of whom led up to Julian of Norwich.

Creation spirituality begins with creation, the universe, nature as a whole. It is not anthropocentric, but first looks at the "whole" beyond merely human interests. It is a tradition honored by indigenous peoples the world over, but the premodern medieval world boasted many teachers operating from a similar mode of consciousness. Consider Thomas Aquinas's teaching that "revelation comes in two volumes—nature and the Bible," which clearly takes the rug out from under those believers who think all of God's teaching will be found in a book. According to Aquinas—and Julian—all of creation is sacred. Creation is also a source of revelation about all that is holy.

How the Plague Killed Creation Spirituality

The plague of Julian's day killed about 25 million people in Europe; it also came close to killing the creation spirituality tradition, as Thomas Berry observes.

> The great shock in Western appreciation of the wild came with the Black Death in the two years 1347–1349, an event that terminated the Medieval Period. A sense of alienation from the natural world was developed at this time. The people had no explanation for what was happening. They knew nothing of germs. They could only figure that the world had grown wicked. God was punishing the world. Confidence in the natural world as the basic mode of divine presence was shaken. A new emphasis was place on redemption out of this world. The grace, compassion and

naturalism in the art of Giotto and Cimabue gave way to the severity of the Last Judgment scene of Michelangelo where Christ is depicted with upraised arm condemning the wicked to everlasting perdition.[4]

As it transitioned from loving nature to fearing it, humanity shrunk its soul and came to see itself in a battle *against* nature. Religion and culture gradually elevated fear of nature over trust in it, eventually making life *after* death more important than life *before* death. An obsessive preoccupation with redemption overtook love of creation in religion. Flagellants emerged who felt the cause of the plague was rampant sinfulness, so they opted physically to beat themselves up to atone for their sins. These groups became so influential as they passed from town to town that eventually the pope forbade them. The price of such anthropocentrism was steep, costing religion and culture far more than anyone must have expected.

When, two hundred years later, Europeans sailed to foreign shores and found indigenous peoples at home with the wonder and sacredness of nature, they accused them of being "savages" while savagely killing them in the millions and ravaging their cultures.

Creation spirituality had already taken two hits in the hundred-year period prior to the Black Death. First, there was the condemnation of Thomas Aquinas in 1276 that followed on his death by bishops at the universities of Paris and Oxford—probably the most influential and respected theology faculties in Europe. In theory, these condemnations were lifted on the canonizing of Aquinas a half-century later, but in many ways that canonization was a speculative rather than practical matter. As Marie-Dominique Chenu put it, "The delayed approval of his theology was destined to make it official rather than practically effective. . . . Christianity was scarcely ever able to effectively oppose the attractions of the dual spiritualism of Augustine and Descartes."[5] Christianity became set up for the very dualism that Aquinas fought all his life. Chenu is saying that when it came to the church at large, he failed.

A second blow to creation spirituality occurred just six years after Aquinas's' canonization, when Pope John XXII condemned Meister Eckhart a week after he died. Eckhart, a disciple of and Dominican brother to Thomas Aquinas, was a mystical teacher and developer of the creation spirituality tradition who had worked closely with the women's movement of Beguines over the years and was a champion for the sacred marriage of nature and grace. Nature *is* grace, Eckhart would say.

The Black Death that waged in Julian's day, then, became a third nail in the coffin of creation spirituality. But what is stunning about Julian is that, despite the momentum against her, she celebrates and develops that tradition even further. For her, like Eckhart, nature *is* grace and grace *is* nature. Trust in nature precedes fear and overcomes it. The body is to be celebrated; sensuality and spirituality form a sacred marriage. Julian is committed to this sacred marriage of nature and grace, humanity and the divine. That is not to say that she ignored the darkness and dark nights of the soul, but she dealt with them in a larger context of the blessing that comprises nature and human life. Julian, too, as is clear in the chapters that follow, champions a non-dualism such as that which Aquinas and Eckhart stood for. All authentic mystics do. Unfortunately, dualism and anthropocentrism, suspicion of science and creation as the source of wonder and wisdom, and preoccupation with human sin continue in religion and culture to carry the day.

After the Black Death uprooted the creation spirituality of the twelfth-century renaissance, creation spirituality was at a premium during the Protestant Reformation. Its scarcity is only underscored by Lutheran and Calvinist pronouncements on the depravity of humans and the fallenness of creation. To be sure, creation spirituality did manage to make its way into the more radical reform movement, as figures such as Hans Hut, Sebastian Frank, Hans Denck, and eventually George Fox (founder of the Quakers) combined action with contemplation, mysticism and prophecy. But creation spirituality also suffered another severe blow with the condemnation, torture, and execution of the ex-Dominican Giordano Bruno, burned at the stake in Rome for daring to bring Copernicus into the world of faith (as his Dominican brother Aquinas had done with Aristotle 300 years prior). His demise became a warning and red flag for those daring to unite science and religion, nature and grace.

My method in this book is to let Julian do as much of the talking as possible. She has much to say, and her feminine voice deserves to be heard, especially at a time when patriarchy and its teachings about dualism and domination, power-over dynamics and knowledge for power's sake, superiority neuroses that revel in empire building, and the pursuit of knowledge at the expense of wisdom have reigned for centuries. These same creeds are revealing themselves as morally bankrupt and dangerous for people, other creatures, and the earth itself in our time. The coronavirus emergency comes wrapped up inside the climate change emergency, for it is part and parcel of the encroaching of the human population onto the habitats of animals.

Julian is a champion of the return of the divine feminine, so much of which has been sidelined since her time (which helps to explain why her work was ignored for centuries). We cannot ignore it any longer if we are to survive as a species. Recovering a healthy balance of the divine feminine and sacred masculine is at the heart of our survival and sustainability as a species, and Julian can lead the way.

One way to talk about wisdom as distinct from knowledge is proposed by the Sufi mystic Rumi who tells us: "Yesterday I was clever, so I wanted to change the world. Today, I am wise, so I am changing myself." Knowledge is clever and knows it—it likes to strut its stuff and it seeks to change others; wisdom is not afraid to look inside and see what needs changing there. It follows, then, that wisdom is more radical than knowledge alone. It dares to ask: "How do I need changing?" The two need not be mutually exclusive, however. It is not an either/or choice between knowledge and wisdom, but a both/and is required—inner and outer work go together. As the late physicist David Bohm put it, "Something more than science is needed." Values are needed, as well as the passion and courage to live them and put them into practice. Julian, who performed her inner work and invites us to do ours, is such a leader of rounded values who offers us a vision for our future.

In this book I welcome Julian to present her guidance for the future that includes both inner and outer work. She does so in the seven chapters that follow. In many ways they might be understood as Julian instructing us in lessons for *enduring, undergoing, and learning from* the coronavirus.

Wisdom does not necessarily grow with time like knowledge does. It can, however, like good wine, become more rich and valuable over time, for so often wisdom is ahead of its time. My experience is that persons introduced to Hildegard, Aquinas, Eckhart, and Julian for the first time are thrilled to hear the wisdom of creation spirituality that they live and teach. This is why, in a time parched for wisdom like ours, when wisdom has been sidelined by academia or education devoted almost exclusively to knowledge, we are invited to return to our ancestors who have proven themselves wise. Julian is such an ancestor. Unlike many believers of her day (and ours), the plague did not plunge her into paroxysms of self-pity, cursing of nature and existence, or despair. In fact, she frequently criticizes those who have given up and fallen into a sickness of sadness and depression (called in her day the capital sin of *acedia*). Julian moves far beyond sadness and urges us to do the same and ground ourselves in ways of empowerment when chaos is all about us. She spells out those ways to ground ourselves in the seven singular chapters in this book.

There were very few copies of Julian's books made. What we possess of her books are handwritten versions, of which only three copies survive. No copies of Julian's book were printed until the seventeenth century, even though the first printing press in England began operation in 1476 with Chaucer's *The Canterbury Tales*. Julian was a contemporary of Chaucer, but of course his works enjoyed exponentially more attention in the centuries that followed.

Julian's work was considered heretical by some, and her being a woman was not considered a mark of credibility in her day. In her first book, she senses the potential controversy her book might provoke, demonstrating "an apprehension of the hostility which her writings may arouse."[6] There was nothing naive about her. Evelyn Underhill called Julian "the first English woman of letters." Julian was certainly one of the pioneers of the English language—in fact, she invented the word *enjoy*. (This is not so unheard of with creation-centered mystics like Francis of Assisi and Dante, both of whom were early writers of the Italian language, as well as Meister Eckhart, who served a similar role in codifying the German language.) When Hildegard, Aquinas, and Eckhart celebrate the artist within us all and talk about our co-creating with God, they mean it—it extends even to developing new languages.

In 1623, two centuries after Julian's death, nine English women left England to start a convent in Holland. They ranged from seventeen to twenty-two years of age, and three of them were descendants of Thomas More (their great, great grandfather). They brought with them from England some manuscripts of Julian's book.

Medieval scholars Edmund Colledge, OSA, and James Walsh, SJ, worked together to edit and translate the *Showings* in a critical edition of the original, old English. They make the point that Julian "was never, until the twentieth century, a popular author" and that she often "startled" her readers.[7] She even anticipated in her first book how antipathy might arise toward her work. Creation spirituality did not match the pessimism of the time of pandemic, nor did it appeal to the empire-building that began with the papal bulls promulgating the doctrine of discovery and Columbus's voyages in the fifteenth century. Nor did it fit with the religious wars of the sixteenth and seventeenth centuries and a patriarchal mindset more influenced by Augustine's sense of original sin than an encounter with the Cosmic Christ. Indeed, Julian's creation spirituality speaks to us today more powerfully than at any time in the past.

One notable nineteenth-century exception to ignorance about her, however, was Florence Nightingale, who read her work and practiced her teachings of mother love by pursuing a nursing vocation and essentially birthing the nursing profession. In the early twentieth century, poet T. S. Eliot incorporated her work into his *Four Quartets*, and one Eliot scholar even says that Julian's teachings—namely, her teaching on how evil can serve a larger purpose—assisted to bring "the thematic thrust of the entire sequence [of *Little Gidding*] to a satisfactory resolution."[8]

The famed twentieth-century Trappist monk Thomas Merton was profoundly excited about Julian of Norwich after his conversion from monastic dualism, a conversion that came about by studying Meister Eckhart in 1958 under the urging of Buddhist teacher Dr. T. J. Suzuki, who brought Zen to North America. In a letter to Sister Mary Madeleva in 1961, the president of St. Mary's College in Notre Dame who had just inaugurated the first advanced degree program in theology for women, Merton exclaims:

Julian is without any doubt one of the most wonderful of all Christian voices. She gets greater and greater in my eyes as I grow older and whereas in the old days I used to be crazy about St. John of the Cross, I would not exchange him now for Julian if you gave me the world and the Indies and all the Spanish mystics rolled up in one bundle. I think that Julian of Norwich is with Newman the greatest English theologian. She is really that. For she reasons from her experience of the substantial center of the great Christian mystery of Redemption. She gives her experience and her deductions clearly, separating the two. And the experience is of course nothing merely subjective. It is the objective mystery of Christ as apprehended by her with the mind and formation of a fourteenth-century English woman.[9]

This is amazing praise, calling Julian "the greatest English theologian" along with Newman. I wholeheartedly agree with Merton here. But his saying that she supplants John of the Cross and other Spanish mystics is even more shocking. Julian developed the theme of the "motherhood of God" more fully than any theologian up to the late twentieth century— and Merton knew that. He too speaks of the "Motherhood of God."[10] For me Julian is very much an heir of Hildegard's, Francis's, Aquinas's, Mechtild's and Eckhart's creation-centered spirituality.

Julian offers us two titles for her book, one is *Showings* and the other is *Revelations of Divine Love*. Of course, neither title nullifies the other— her showings are revelations or illuminations. And the subject matter of these showings, revelations and illuminations can be summarized as *divine love*—a love that Julian sees everywhere in creation and within the human soul. She insists that we must do inner work, including dying and letting go to come to grips with love all over again. Our outer worlds and our response to everyday events can conceal or distort our inner and deepest self, and so we must "dig and ditch" (Julian's words) to recover it.

Julian tells us that her sixteen revelations came to her on May 8, 1373, when she was "a simple, unlearned creature" at age thirty. This language is often a kind of formality for medieval women to utter (even the accomplished Hildegard of Bingen said something similar), so it ought not be taken at full value. Obviously, Julian was literate, and most men and women of her day were not, so she was not as "unlearned" as she claims. (In fact, Colledge and Walsh call her a "learned woman" and a "great scholar.")[10] The fuller version of her book that came decades later, Julian describes this way. "Fifteen showings which God delivered to my consciousness, renewed by illuminations and inspirations from, I hope, the same spirit that revealed them all those years ago." Then she goes on to tell us how they began at 4 a.m. and lasted until 3 p.m., "unfolding one after the other in the most elegant order, in deep quietude." And the next night came the sixteenth vision, which "completed and confirmed the previous fifteen."[i] Thus she assigns her later reflections the same level of importance as the original revelations themselves.

She goes on to say that she had prayed for three things: to participate in the sufferings of Jesus, to undergo a "life-threatening illness" (likely the plague), and to experience "the grace of the triple-wound of contrition, compassion, and unbearable longing." Her prayers were indeed answered, and she got very sick. So close was she to death that her friends called a priest to administer the last rites. "I yearned to fully experience all the discomfort of dying—physical and mental—with the accompanying terror and temptations of the spirits of evil. I wished to go to the brink of death, but not pass over. What I wanted was for this sickness to purify me, so that, by the grace of God, I would live more fully for his sake alone. Also, I was hoping it would prepare me for my real death, which I anticipated would soon be coming. I was ready to return to my God and Maker."[ii]

Instead of dying literally, however, she underwent a kind of death and with it a kind of resurrection like what Thomas Aquinas calls the "first resurrection"—that is, an experience of "waking up" in this lifetime. Some might call it enlightenment, others breakthrough, or *satori*.

We do not know much about Julian's life story other than that she lived through the bubonic plague, and she clearly had a special mother who helped see her through the pandemic as a child and left a deep impression

---

[i] Mirabai Starr, *The Showings of Julian of Norwich: A New Translation* (Charlottesville, VA: Hampton Roads Publishing Company, Inc., 2013), 180. Henceforth, abbreviated as S.

[ii] S 6f.

on her about what authentic motherhood is all about—lessons about trust that Julian develops in her rich theology of the motherhood of God. Mirabai Starr raises the possibility that Julian may have been a wife and mother herself, one who lost her family to the bubonic plague. Colledge and Walsh suggest that she may have gone to France to be educated as a young woman.

There is strong evidence that Julian was educated by the Benedictines, as she was clearly a knowledgeable woman—and for centuries the Benedictines had excelled at educating girls. She is steeped in a consciousness of wisdom that is integral to the training of Benedictine sisters, including the practice of singing the psalms (part of the biblical wisdom tradition).

In Julian's day the Dominican Order was strong in Norwich. They had arrived in England in 1221, just six years after the foundation of the order by St. Dominic. Dominicans came to Norwich in 1226, just three years after Aquinas's canonization. One can only imagine how excited they were to be preaching his theology, newly embraced by the church at large, after being under a shadow of suspicion for decades following his condemnations (in fact, Franciscans had been forbidden to read Aquinas's *Summa Theologiae*—that is how deeply threatening some held Aquinas to be). In 1307 the Dominicans took over the Penitential Friars' building in Norwich and its large library when that order was suppressed by Pope Clement V.

There is reason to believe that the influence of Dominicans Thomas Aquinas and Meister Eckhart was considerable on Julian. It is, in fact, quite possible that one or more Dominicans may have served as her spiritual director, as one had done for Mechtild of Magdeburg.

Julian as Anchoress

Julian chose not to live in a monastery as an adult but became an anchoress, living more or less as a hermit, or religious recluse, in a cell attached to a church. An anchoress attended Mass regularly from her cell with a small window into the chapel to receive communion. The cell also had a window to the outside, through which she would offer counsel and instruction to those seeking spiritual advice. While undergoing a symbolic "leaving the world" and "death to the world" in a ceremonial ritual conducted by a bishop upon moving into her cell, and vowing to remain until death, nevertheless an anchoress might be very much in demand and even at the center of a community if they were well known and respected. Most likely that was the case with Julian.

An anchoress usually had a companion or two who would assist her. We know the names of two of Julian's helpers: Sara and Alice. Their responsibilities would include bringing food and drink, probably helping with laundry and messages, bringing books to read and providing paper and pen for writing, and surely also emptying the chamber pot. This detail is especially important in Julian's case since, as noted in chapter 6, she extols the spiritual dimension of going to the bathroom.

The anchorite tradition traces its beginnings to the third and fourth centuries in Palestine. Men were called anchorites, and there were far fewer of them than there were women. In England, the first recorded examples date to the eleventh century. About two hundred anchorites peopled England in the thirteenth century. The COVID-19 pandemic has forced a stay-at-home policy and a quarantine as much as possible, so it seems especially fitting to be keeping company with a woman who did this full-time for most of her adult life. Surely Julian has much to teach us today about how to navigate a time of enclosure in a time of a plague.

Julian's cell was destroyed by bombing in World War II, though it has since been rebuilt, and I have enjoyed the privilege to visit it. I was struck, first of all, by how ordinary and unpretentious the church was. Three women, one of whom was Jewish, and I celebrated a modest Mass within her cell. Among other prayers, we created mantras of some of Julian's wonderful teachings, and we chanted them over and over. For example, "Goodness is God" or "all will be well," and so on.

Secondly, I was struck how the cell bordered along a walkway coming up from the river a short distance away. There is no question that sailors (some more sober than others, no doubt) may have stopped by her window at all times of day and night, having disembarked from either their skiff or their taverns. I think that helps to account for how down-to-earth Julian's writings are. She was not holed away in a monastery out in the countryside but located in the midst of human traffic in a town with a busy waterway. I found her church, after which she is named, to be very plain—not unlike her, in fact. I salute those in England for keeping it that way (and positioning a gift shop with books and memorabilia on Julian a short distance away from the church itself).

Clearly Julian enjoyed a lively intellectual and imaginative life. Like Hildegard two centuries before her, she praises learning and "reason" when she says, "I saw that our Reason is in God, and it is the highest gift we have received. It is grounded in nature."[i] This very much echoes her sister Hildegard, who declared that "our greatest treasure is a living intellect" and "all science comes from God." Hildegard taught that humans can understand "all things" because we possess the gift of rationality or intellect. Indeed, for Hildegard, Christ was "Holy Rationality" itself, and she asserted that "God is Rationality." To study scripture or anything else is to employ rationality, which "leads the human being's five senses to God's righteousness."[11]

Julian's fine Benedictine education and her love of the intellectual life was nurtured as an adult most likely when she encountered one or more Dominicans, who introduced her to the theology of Thomas Aquinas and Meister Eckhart. Some of Eckhart's writings had been smuggled into England in books under John Tauler's name. Tauler was a Dominican student of Eckhart who had not been condemned (medieval Dominicans were quite canny defending their own).

But above all, she stayed true to her visions at thirty years of age, mining them throughout her life for their wisdom and the message and meaning they relayed not only for herself but for others. She was very much at home with her womanhood and her body and was probably considered a holy woman in her time to whom many people, men (sailors included) and women, ordinary and of some noble classes, came for spiritual direction and counsel. She had tremendous self-confidence (we devote a chapter below to her teachings on trust) that bolstered her to write what was in effect three books.

A singular characteristic about her writing is that in her books she cites very few theologians or even biblical texts. Having learned to integrate her readings thoroughly into her own thinking and with years of contemplative study, she creates her own theology. She learns to trust her own experience, especially the revelations themselves, and she spends

---

[i] Brendan Doyle, *Meditations with Julian of Norwich* (Santa Fe, NM: Bear & Co., 1983), 132. Henceforth abbreviated as D.

decades following her first book unpacking them them for the wisdom they contain. She recognizes that the showings are "full of secrets" and hold layers of meaning that it takes her years of deciphering to arrive at "the full teaching," which she comes to "understand over time."[i] To be sure, she integrates biblical stories and teachings as well as those of other theologians in her writing, but she is primarily turning her showings over and over in her mind and heart and applying them to her life experience and interactions with others. The bottom line is that she shares, trusts, and exegetes her experience, and that is what her second and third books are all about. In doing so, she creates a fresh theological vision and invites the reader to participate by trusting their own experience. Here, too, she speaks to us today as we need fresh visions of spirituality by which to serve the world.

That she was a profound thinker and practitioner of the lineage of creation spirituality cannot be denied. All the more stunning is that she lays out her case for the goodness and grace of nature during a time of pandemic when so many were turning their backs on ever trusting nature again. In Julian's day, people drew very different conclusions from the pandemic–namely, that nature hates us, that God is punishing us, and that humans are so guilty and full of shame that sin is the biggest truth about humanity. In short, they lost creation spirituality, as Thomas Berry says. Julian did not go down this theological rabbit hole, however, and this makes her so unlike the Protestant reformers and much of Christianity that followed even to our day.

While she has much to teach us in our time of self-enclosure during our twenty-first-century pandemic, she has just as much to teach us after the pandemic is over. Her teachings and insights are by no means restricted to a time of pandemic—in fact, our meditating on them and implementing them might well help to prevent pandemics in the future. She inspires us to face our own extinction that is coming with climate change bearing down on us.

---

[i] S 132.

Another dimension to Julian's thought is its deep humanism and deep ecumenism or interfaith. This should not surprise us since wisdom literature even in the Bible is very ecumenical. The queen of Sheba, after all, is African and not Jewish, and when you put nature or creation out front as a source of revelation (as wisdom literature and creation spirituality does), you necessarily are prone to greater inclusion. As I wrote in my first book on the Cosmic Christ, there is no such thing as a Buddhist river, a Roman Catholic ocean, a Baptist moon, or an atheist cornfield.

Julian makes explicit on many occasions that she is speaking to a very broad audience—one that includes those of us who live 650 years later. It follows, then, that we recognize that sense of inclusion. "In God's sight, all humanity is one person, and all people are a single humanity."[i] She sees Christ as an embodiment of humanity itself. "This is what I understood about Christ's human aspect: Christ himself embodies all humanity."[ii] If Christ offers liberation to any, he offers it to all humans. "His sweet incarnation and blessed passion will liberate us all, because he is our head and we all the parts of his body."[iii] For Julian, the traditional teaching of the church as the mystical body of Christ is extended to the entire human race. Moreover, "Christ represents the spiritual yearning in us all. Christ is all spiritual seekers, and all spiritual seekers are Christ."[iv] Here Julian is invoking the Cosmic Christ, who is found in all beings and in all human beings.

When she celebrates the beauty of being human, she again makes explicit that she is talking about *all* and not some sectarian group. "God made us so rich and noble in our essence that all we can do is strive to enact his will and honor him in all things. When I say 'we,' I mean all true spiritual seekers."[v] When she says "all," she means all. This would include, in our time, all versions of Christians and all Jews, all Buddhists, Hindus, Taoists, Muslims, goddess worshippers, those of indigenous religions, and

---

[i] S 133.
[ii] S 139.
[iii] S 139.
[iv] S 139.
[v] S 157.

those of no religions whether agnostic or atheist. That is how ecumenical she is—and in the fourteenth century, no less.

When speaking of retreating "into our own souls, which is where our Beloved dwells," she again speaks out about the universality that encompasses our spiritual search: "Let no man or woman think this truth applies personally to the individual. It does not; it is universal. This beautiful human nature of ours was prepared for our precious Mother Christ. Since before the beginning she recognized, knew, and understood that humanity was created for God's honor and glory, and for the utter joy and bliss of our salvation."[i] Again, Julian thinks and expresses herself in the context of the whole, of the universality of the human condition, of our carrying within us "this beautiful human nature of ours."

In explaining how she came to write her book, she confesses that she first saw them as a personal thing, but then she came to understand they applied to humanity *as a whole*. "At first, I applied this teaching to my individual self, because at the time I was not moved to see it otherwise. But the great and gracious comfort that followed made me realize that God meant this insight *for the whole of humanity*." She learned that her work ought to reach a broad audience, "I made the mistake of privatizing this showing instead of taking it to mean loving my fellow Christians better. What could make me love my fellow Christians better than to see that God loves us all as we are all one soul?"[ii] She adds a note about learning to judge others less: "I was reminded too that I must not focus on the imperfections of others but instead take responsibility for my own. The only exception to this would be if my reflections could be helpful and comforting to my fellow spiritual seekers."[iii]

Such a sense of universality translates into action, for "those who have universal love for all their fellow Christians in God have love towards everything that exists. For in us all is comprehended all, that is, all that is created and the Creator of all." Creation and the cosmos belong to everyone—and no one—and it calls us to a larger consciousness of expanded love.[iv]

---

[i] S 172.

[ii] D 64.

[iii] S 212.

[iv] D 33.

Julian speaks often of God "resting in the human soul." But near the end of her book, she extends that image to a less individual and more universal image when she says: *"He has chosen the soul of humanity as his resting place,* and this is the great city and honorable throne from which he lovingly reigns. He will never rise or move away from this spot inside us. What a wondrous and magnificent place it is where the Beloved dwells!"[i]

Early in her book, she speaks to her audience—which she makes clear is a broad one—when she tells her readers, "I was moved by a deep love for my fellow spiritual seekers, praying that they could all see what I was seeing, because I knew it would be such a comfort to them."[ii] Here she explains her motive for writing: "I understood that the vision I was receiving was not for me alone, *but for all.*"

One must not fail to recognize what a powerful political stand Julian makes when she insists on her book being universal and for all. After all, one of the popular responses to the Black Death was to create scapegoats—namely, "heretics" or Jews. Indeed, antisemitism abounded during the pandemic as people looked for someone to blame. Many Jews fled England. But there is not an ounce of anti-semitism or heresy attacks in any of Julian's books. She also utterly rejects the notion that personal sins were the cause of the pandemic (a mentality that, again, found expression in the flagellation movements). As we shall see in chapter six, she stood up fiercely to those who wanted to separate spirituality and sensuality and disparage the latter. In fact, the whole discussion on "sin" rises often in Julian's book, and she prefers to say that our mistakes often lead to a greater good, and that sin is overrated. Instead of focusing on sin, she advises us to focus more on our better natures and the grace that is found there.

Julian refers to herself as a "simple" person, and she is certain that "there are many people who have never had visions and yet love God far better than I do." But she is thinking of the larger community for "when I look at myself as an individual, I see that I am nothing. It is only in unity with my fellow spiritual seekers that I am anything at all. It is this foundation of unity that will save humanity."[iii] Again, "humanity" is on her mind in writing and sharing this book. That includes us who come

---

[i] S 216.

[ii] S 22.

[iii] S 23.

to her for guidance and wisdom in the twenty-first century as we endure a pandemic of our own.

Translations for this Book

I am indebted to Edmund Colledge, OSA, and James Walsh, SJ, for their two-volume critical edition of Julian's medieval manuscripts.[12] While that edition has been invaluable to my own understanding of Julian, I have chosen two more contemporary translations of Julian's work to employ in this book. The first is from Mirabai Starr, whose love and understanding of the mystics comes from a very deep place. Grounded in that love of the mystics, she is herself committed to ecumenism and her translations of John of the Cross and Teresa of Ávila demonstrate her sensitivity to the world of the mystics. Starr's *The Showings of Julian of Norwich: A New Translation* is one of the two books I utilize. Living in the twenty-first century and in a world of interfaith, she has wisely chosen to translate Julian with a sensitivity that moves beyond religious sectarianism. For example, she has changed Julian's term of "my even Christians" to "my fellow spiritual seekers," and sometimes she translates "our faith" and "the church" as "our spiritual community." Similarly, "those who will be saved" become "all beings"; the "devil" becomes "the spirit of evil"; and "sin" becomes "missing the mark" or "error," "transgression," "imperfection," or "negativity." Starr recognizes the importance of Julian's message reaching the entire world, rather than being hoarded by religionists of one stripe, when she remarks that Julian's work is "for the sake of all spiritual seekers everywhere."[13]

Another great quote of Starr's is: "I don't just want my translations to be 'true'; I want them to be beautiful—a pleasure to read, a heart-opening encounter."[14] Indeed! The mystics deserve this. Mystics should be translated by other mystics, for far too long academics have handed down translations that fall woefully short and remain tainted by dualisms and patriarchal mindsets. Few academics have stayed in touch with their mystical roots. Julian, a champion of the divine feminine, deserves a female translator, and Mirabai Starr rose to the occasion. She wonderfully captures the spirit and meaning of Julian by her sensitive language and her own mystical grounding.

A second translation I have invoked is from Brendan Doyle's *Meditations with Julian of Norwich*, which appeared in 1983 firmly grounded in the tradition of creation spirituality.[15] It was my privilege both to oversee the publication of Doyle's translation by the publishing house I founded and to write a foreword to that book. I believe his translation has very much stood the test of time, for Brendan worked from the critical edition of Julian's medieval text and diligently translated with sensitivity, care, and an understanding of the tradition she so marvelously represents—that of creation spirituality. He frequently chose to translate "salvation" as "liberation," because Thomas Aquinas does exactly that when he writes *salvatio seu liberatio* (*seu* means "or" as in *a synonym for*). Brendan, being a musician, brought a musical intuition to his translations. He was also a student and well-respected teacher at both the Institute in Culture and Creation Spirituality at Mundelein College, Chicago, and at ICCS in Holy Names College, Oakland, California where he was a beloved administrator as well. On a final note, I was thrilled to see this translation on display at the Julian Centre near her church in Norwich when I visited there.

To both of these translators who have done so much to bring Julian alive and real in our day, I say *thank you!* Because this book emphasizes Julian's own words, and to make references as inobtrusive as possible, I have chosen to footnote Julian's words from these two texts at the bottom of each page by way of roman numerals. I abbreviate them as "D" (Doyle) and "S" (Starr). Citations for other sources are provided in endnotes.

Seven Lessons for Thriving Spiritually in a Time of Pandemic

I've organized this book according to seven distinct lessons that Julian shares with us to navigate a pandemic and grow spiritually in the process.

Chapter 1 instructs us not to flee the darkness but to stick around for everything that the suffering, chaos, un-knowing, and the dark night of the soul have to teach us.

Chapter 2 instructs us not to forget the deep-down goodness of things and that pervades existence itself, which should elicit joy, awe, and wonder. Julian stayed true to her philosophy of goodness—indeed her *metaphysic of goodness*—while living side-by-side, day in and day out, with the bubonic plague. She practiced what she preached; she walked her talk.

Chapter 3 calls us to deep reflection on and appreciation of the divinity to be found in nature as a whole (the cosmos), as well as in creatures and all beings that dwell in nature. There are echoes in this teaching to be found in the work of Emily Dickinson, who we might say in her own day and in her own way underwent a kind of "anchoress" lifestyle. Dickinson, for example, offers us a nature-based Trinitarian blessing: "in the name of the bee, the butterfly and the breeze."

Chapter 4 urges the return of the divine feminine and a deep sense of the motherhood of God. Julian demands that we bring gender balance alive in our souls, our institutions, and our culture. The way we educate, for example—is it a search for wisdom (which is feminine)? Or is it a rabid quest for knowledge, and with it raw power over nature, over others, and over our own hearts? By inviting in the feminine dimension of divinity, Julian calls for a time of gender balance and a return of health.

Chapter 5 calls us to our deepest selves, our most noble selves, our truest selves, and therefore to an experience of non-dualism between us and the divine. Thomas Aquinas taught that "God became human in order that humans might become divine," and Julian agrees with him. Are we there yet? What holds us back?

Chapter 6 addresses the primacy of trust and courage—including trust in our own bodiliness and earthiness. Our sensuality, sexuality, and spirituality come together to make a sacred marriage—and non-dualism can grace all our relations. Courage and magnanimity are born of this same trust.

Chapter 7 reminds us how Love unites us all. Not a sentimental love, however, as Julian actually calls us to do battle with sentimentality. She encourages us to stand up to the forces that destroy, forces she calls "the spirit of evil." As we face uncertainty and deep darkness as discussed in chapter 1, we also come to the realization that the shadow, the "fiend," or the destructive side of Kali stalks us inside and outside, in our dreams and in our institutions, in our inner lives and our outer work, in politics and in economics. This "spirit of evil" includes not only matricide to Mother Earth but misogyny to women everywhere. But the warrior in us can rise up, armed with trust and courage, to spread love and make justice and compassion happen. In doing this, a promise is set forth that, some day, all can be well.

Chapter 8 summarizes the foundational teachings found in the previous seven chapters. There is so much richness in Julian's showings, and they are not at all presented in a linear way. She tends to think in such a spiral (almost musical) fashion, returning to themes and expanding them along the way, that I find it useful to list them so we understand and remember them more easily in this chapter.

In the conclusion and epilogue we take a deeper look at how Julian is speaking directly to us today about issues of pandemic, climate change, sexism, misogyny, matricide, and patriarchy. We recognize her mystical voice reaching a crescendo as a prophetic voice. We also come up against the racist and genocidal history of the West encapsulated in the Doctrine of Discovery papal bulls promulgated in the fifteenth century by two popes. What if, instead of demanding redemption of non-Christian peoples in Africa and the Americas, the European explorers had put the goodness of creation at the forefront of their spirituality? How different would history have been if Julian's religious vision which leads with the goodness of creation prompted the encounters between Europe and indigenous peoples the worldover?

Julian of Norwich is a mystic-prophet for our time who offers us a quiet but profound revolution in consciousness and practice, even as we all undergo the vicissitudes of confronting a deadly pandemic. She faced the same reality after all, with far fewer resources than we have at our disposal, throughout her lifetime and she took advantage of the crisis to explore more deeply what her soul and heart truly desired and was capable of. That is what mystics do—and we are all mystics, especially in a time of radical transformation such as this.

The truths that she laid out are gathered, I hope faithfully, in the chapters that follow. Our sister and ancestor Julian is eager not only to speak to us today but *to shout at us*—albeit in a gentle way—to wake up and to go deep, to face the darkness and to dig down and find goodness, joy and awe. And to go to work to defend Mother Earth and all her creatures, stripping ourselves of racism, sexism, nationalisms, anthropocentrism, sectarianism—anything that interferes with our greatness as human beings. And to connect anew to the sacredness of life.

Recently, while teaching a course on Thomas Aquinas and researching his mentor, the scientist, philosopher and theologian, St. Albert the Great

(1193–1280), I ran across a German historian of science who proclaimed that if the church had followed Albert's approach and respect for science, Western culture would have launched modern science four hundred years earlier.

I might propose, after fifty years of researching, writing, and teaching the creation spirituality tradition, that if the church had chosen to follow Julian of Norwich and the lineage that she heralds, neither the Protestant Reformation nor the Catholic Counter-Reformation would have been necessary—not to mention the religious wars, imperial invasions, and decimations of indigenous people that followed. I dare to say that even the two world wars of the twentieth century could have been avoided, as well as the devastating matricide toward Mother Earth that we have witnessed since the rise of industrialization.

That is how much transformation Julian's example of a return of the divine feminine and a balance of the feminine and heathy masculine can achieve. One can hope that Julian's deep feminism and love of nature attracts the future of spirituality, now that our species faces not only a deadly pandemic but an even more deadly climate change emergency that, along with other calamities and extinctions, will bring even more viruses along with it. Only such a quiet revolution will ensure her mighty vision might some day come true and that "all might be well."

1

FACING THE DARKNESS

Sometimes we experience such darkness that we lose all our energy.—Julian

A time of pandemic is a time of much darkness. First, there is the darkness of not knowing when it will end—this was surely the case in the fourteenth century, when a science of viruses and pathogens did not exist and the bubonic plague seemed to come out of the blue. Also, because the plague came in waves, there was always the fear that it would return. Each wave left another set of questions behind: Is it gone? Will it return? Will life ever get back to normal?

Today we feel many of these same feelings and pose similar questions, but we have light on the horizon in the form of medical science. We assume that scientists will find a vaccine, but questions remain: How long will it take? How effective will it be? How universally will it be distributed? How swiftly will that happen? What will it cost? Will the poor have access to it?

Secondly, there is the darkness of knowing that suffering and death are happening all around us, yet we can do very little about it except to stay indoors, self-isolate, wear masks in public, and support those working on the front lines. There is also darkness in *not* knowing who is carrying the virus. The media and social media keep us abreast of the numbers of cases, the burdens on our hospitals and caregivers, the number of deaths, pictures of portable morgues and tent hospitals to house all the sick and dying—and this leads to anxiety, fear, and deep sadness.

The darkness of *not-knowing* about a virus is stacked upon other

1

realities of non-knowing, as even before the coronavirus hit, our species was already facing apocalyptic happenings. Reports from the United Nations written by scientists from around the world alerted us to the catastrophe of a climate change that continues to bear down on us more swiftly and severely than we had suspected. In 2019, the United Nations reported we had ten years to change our ways as a species or the melting of glaciers and rising of seas would overwhelm us beyond measure. The melting of glaciers, rising of the seas, burning of rainforests, increased droughts, swelling number and severity of hurricanes and floods, increasing temperatures, and intensified migrations delivered a similar message. Meanwhile, an entire continent, Australia, was on fire. More than the proverbial "canary in the coal mine," we now have *an entire continent* in the mine, so to speak, chirping loudly: "Wake up! Climate change is real. And it is severe beyond belief. Get moving!"

Indeed, the coronavirus is part of the larger crisis of climate change since, like the AIDS virus that killed over 38 million humans worldwide, this virus is derived from interaction between humans and other species. In the case of AIDS, it was human interaction with a monkey in Africa; in the case of the coronavirus, it was interaction with bats in China. The scientific consensus is that the bubonic plague was brought about by rats in medieval Europe, eventually killing one out of every two to three people.

Because the human population has exploded and displaced so many of the habitats of other species, we have endured both AIDS and now the coronavirus. And, scientists warn us, there will be more such dangers even after (and if) the coronavirus is stopped. Levi Sucre Romero, a Bribri indigenous teacher from Costa Rica who coordinates the Mesoamerican Alliance of Peoples and Forests, warns that "the coronavirus is now telling the world what we have been saying for thousands of years—that if we do not help protect biodiversity and nature, then we will face this and worse future threats."[1]

The Dark Night of Our Species

The mystics have a name for all of this bad news: the *via negativa*. This "negative way" is the reality of suffering, death, not-knowing, and not being in control. When the dark side of life gets severe and penetrates our consciousness it is called the "dark night of the soul." Rabbi Heschel alerted us to think and speak not just of the "dark night of the soul" but also the "dark night of society," and he thereby urged us to apply mystical language not just to the depth experiences of individuals but also to the depth experiences of our communities.

I would go even further today, however. Because our species has become so unified and interactive through the internet and social media, so interconnected in finance and transportation and the sharing of ideas and news, we should also be talking about the *dark night of our species.* After all, we face a failing planet and the extinction of more species than at any time in the past 65 million years. And all of humanity is facing the coronavirus.

Our troubles are global. Extinction is happening. Humans are not exempt. We do not have all the answers or a lot of time to change things around. Thus, the dark night of our species is upon us.

Did Julian and her contemporaries experience a dark night of the soul and society? Surely they did. But few responded with the wisdom she left us. What is that wisdom that she offers us, borne of what she and her contemporaries underwent as they faced one of the most apocalyptic moments in Western history?

She talks about our being sucked of all our energy by the struggles and hardships in life when she writes: "Sometimes we experience such darkness that we lose all our energy." She is speaking here of the depression that burdens can bring upon us and of the capital sin of *acedia*, which Aquinas defines as a "loss of energy to begin new things" that derives from a deep sadness, especially about spiritual things. She talks of our being "borne down by the weight of our mortal flesh" and how "because of this darkness, allowing and trusting God's great love and keeping providence is almost impossible."[i] The deep sadness is real, and it has become a sign of our times. The poet Rainer Maria Rilke says that sometimes we feel like we are carrying the whole weight of the world upon our shoulders.

What to do? One thing to do is to examine our goals and intentions, advises Julian. We should use the occasion to strip everything down to the essential questions: Why am I here? What/whom do I wish to serve? This is how she responds to our dark moments: "But our intent in life

---

[i] D 118.

is to continue to live in God and faithfully trust that we will be shown compassion and grace." Our intent and purpose is itself our co-creation with God. "This is God's own working in us."[i]

Another of Julian's teachings to be learned from a pandemic is this: that life is short. Pandemics remind us that we are all mortal. "God wants us to remember that life is short."[ii] To remember this, of course, is to refuse to go into denial about death or be so preoccupied with trivia that we forget to ask the deeper questions: What do I want to do with my life? What is the best contribution I can make, given my particular gifts and background and not knowing how long I will live?

These might seem like obvious questions, but in a society like ours—one that can easily take our security and comfort for granted—they are not as pressing as they ought to be. In a less sterile society than ours (such as Julian's), death was more starkly near even when times were good. More often than not, people were born at home and died at home. The undertaking industry, whose job it is to paint over the faces of the dead and preserve a body as if it were still alive, did not exist. Death was allowed to be death. And children and citizens of all ages were familiar with it—especially in a time of pandemic.

When I was twelve years old, I underwent an education about the shortness of life that subsequently played a significant role in my life. I contracted polio during a summer vacation that our family took driving from our home in Madison, Wisconsin, to my mother's family in Pennsylvania, and then to New York City and on to Niagara Falls. On the way home we stopped at a beach at Lake Michigan near Gary, Indiana. A few weeks later I was not feeling myself, so I was taken to a hospital where a spinal tap confirmed that I had contracted polio. I was immediately put into the hospital and quarantined, and my siblings were forbidden to visit me, though they could stand outside my first-floor window to visit on occasion. Doctors later traced my polio virus to that beach excursion toward the end of our vacation.

My polio struck me in 1952, one year before the polio vaccine was invented. Polio was a very scary thing in those days— a friend in my neighborhood had died of it the previous summer. In my case, it attacked

---

[i] D 86.

[ii] S 116.

my legs, and the doctor could not tell me whether I would ever walk again. My grandfather on my father's side had contracted polio as a young man, around the age of thirty, and lost his small business repairing vacuum cleaners. He was confined to a wheelchair for the rest of his life.

I learned many things from polio. One was to let go—I was out of school for many months, and friends could not visit. My father had been a football coach at the University of Wisconsin, my older brothers were star football players in high school, and here I was, in eighth grade, being told I may not walk again. I think it is safe to say that I learned to let go of any unconscious projections I harbored about defining myself and my manhood by way of football. In a certain sense, I left my father at that age. Looking back on it, I see polio as a sort of initiation experience.

Many years later, when I was a young Dominican priest, twenty-nine years old and studying in Paris, my mother came to visit, and she told me an amazing story. She said that my father was deeply afraid when I contacted polio, one reason being how the disease had so thoroughly affected his own father's life and work. But he was stunned by how bravely I took the news. "Up till then," she said, "your father only respected physical courage. But you taught him moral courage." So I guess I can say that was another gift from polio.

I received many cards of support, and a Dominican lay brother who served in my parish church visited regularly. I was touched by his deep quietness. The dimension of contemplation as another model for manhood had an effect on me. He later became a Trappist monk.

But the biggest gift of all from my bout with polio occurred after many months in the hospital, when the doctor said that I would, in fact, be able to walk again. I was overwhelmed by the good news, and I recall saying to the universe: "I will never take my legs for granted again."

This is a very mystical statement—indeed, it is one way that I define mysticism, as a state of mind that one does not take for granted. Even each breath is something that we can be aware of and not take for granted. There is a word for such attention to breathing: *meditating*.

I trace my vocation as a Dominican, priest, and a student and teacher of spirituality to the *via negativa* experience of losing my legs as a teenager. Part of not taking things for granted is the *gratitude and reverence* that comes when one realizes what one has, and that includes existence itself and life and good health and a body all of whose parts work well.

I see in Julian's story a somewhat parallel experience. She clearly underwent a deep initiation in the time of a frightening pandemic that was all around her. One Jungian therapist calls her trial and subsequent revelations a kind of shamanistic initiation. Clearly, she underwent a kind of annihilation or dying, from which she returned to tell us of lessons learned from her dying and resurrecting. She describes it in vivid terms:

> When I was thirty and a half years old, God sent me that illness I had asked for in my youth. For three days and three nights I lay in bed, and on the fourth night I was given the last rites of Holy Church. No one expected me to live through the night, yet I lingered for another two days. I kept thinking I was about to die, and everyone who sat with me thought so also.
>
> I was still young enough to be sad about dying. It's not that anything here on earth pleased me (it did not), or that I was afraid of pain (I trusted in his mercy). Rather, I would have liked to live longer simply so that I could have learned to love God better. . . . It suddenly seemed to me that my time here on earth had been so short in comparison to life everlasting that it hardly counted at all.[i]

Her bodily pain and "my own common sense, led me to conclude that yes, my life was over." Her body felt dead from the waist down; she "couldn't feel a thing." A priest arrived and put a crucifix in front of her face. Her sight failed, as "everything grew dim, until the whole room was as dark as night." Only the cross was visible and illuminated in "a rather ordinary light." Next, "the upper part of my body began to die. Soon I had almost no feeling left," and she became short of breath with "the sense that my life was rapidly waning. By this time I was convinced that I was passing away."

But "suddenly all my pain vanished, and I was whole again," feeling "better than I ever had before. . . . This abrupt transformation astonished me." Then she encountered the crucified Christ, and "all of a sudden, I

---

i S 8–12.

saw the red blood trickling down from under his garland of thorns." There followed a presence of Mary who was "very young—a simple, humble girl."[i]

Thus we learn of the setting for her showings: her dying or near-death experience—and her subsequent resurrection. Julian's near-death experience was not focused on an experience of light as such—but on death. That of Jesus but, as she explicitly tells us, he stands for her as "everyman" or humanity as a whole. This suggests that her experience with death around her due to the plague from the age of seven was the starting point for her awakening.

Did Julian lose many friends and relatives? Mirabai Starr suggests that she may have been married with children and have lost her entire family. That might be hinted at when she writes of profound grief this way. "Of all pains that lead to liberation the worst is to see your loved one suffer. How could any pain be more excruciating than to see the one who is all my life, all my happiness and all my joy suffer? The greater, the more able and the sweeter the love is, the more grief it is to the lover to see the body of the loved one in pain."[ii] And she follows up with this observation: "It is natural for the child not to despair of the mother's love. It is natural for the child not to be overconfident. It is natural for the child to love the mother and each brother and sister."[iii] Is this a mother talking? Again, "I understand no higher state in this life than childhood with its minimum of capability and skill unto the time that our gracious Mother has led us to our Father's joy." Might these be the words of a mother who lost her children and has tasted deep grief? And this: "I understood that all the blessed children who come out of God by Nature will be returned into God by Grace."[iv]

The *via negativa* and deep loss remind us all not to take things for granted. A pandemic teaches us the same. A pandemic is a time—and hopefully this applies to post-pandemic life as well—in which we learn not to take things for granted, to be still, and in that process re-evaluate our lives and our culture. The response to the cold-blooded murder of George Floyd, for instance, has also done exactly that. His loss of life quickly

---

[i] S 8–12.

[ii] D 43.

[iii] D 110.

[iv] D 111.

became a rallying cry for the Black Lives Matter Movement, whereby we are learning not only not to take black lives for granted, but to get busy dismantling an overwhelming set of social forces, structures, and attitudes.

Julian's first lesson about a dark night is to face it for what it is. *Do not give in to denial.* Put truth first. Go into the dark, even the darkest of the dark. Go into the dying. Julian acknowledges that sometimes "all our frailties and failings, our betrayals and denials, our humiliations and burdens and all our woe" seem to "utterly fill the horizons of this life."[i] She herself confesses to experiencing "a constant flow of woe here" in this life.[ii] She talks of the "depths of the night" that causes "our pain and woe."[iii]

She describes our woe by asserting that sometimes "the heart is dry and feels nothing, or maybe is being tempted by the spirit of evil to give up on God."[iv] We are stuck; all we feel is the absence of God, a darkness inside and outside us. Indeed, we "see so much evil around us, so much harm done, that we think it impossible that there is any good in this world." Goodness seems gone and out the window, forgotten. "We look at this in sorrow and mourn so that we cannot see God as we should." But she critiques our blindness and shortsightedness when she says: "This is because we use our reason so blindly, so unfully and so simplemindedly that we are unable to know the marvelous wisdom, capability and goodness of the joyful Trinity."[v] We lack perspective. We pay too much attention to the bad news. Joy is part of the big picture, as we shall see in the following chapter. Julian cautions us time and time again not to lose touch with the truth of the goodness of life and of nature even in the most dire of conditions.

I recall the morning of September 11, 2011: our University of Creation Spirituality was in session. An indigenous elder who happened to be visiting that day told us: "In our tradition, when a great trauma has happened, we are encouraged not to dwell on it. Address it directly, but do not keep turning it over and over in your head—like the media is doing playing over and over the film of the planes crashing into the towers in New York

---

[i] S 171.
[ii] S 176.
[iii] S 220.
[iv] S 101.
[v] D 56.

City." I think the same advice applies to our coronavirus emergency. Facts are important, but dwelling incessantly on the damage can be debilitating.

Julian counsels grief work as well: "Both reason and grace drive the soul to cry out to the Lord, imploring him in a loud voice, recalling his blessed passion and his great goodness." With that kind of howling, that way of expressing our deep grief, something can shift in us, so that sometimes we move from darkness to light. "And so the power of our Lord's word enters the soul and enlivens the heart. By his grace, we begin to engage in true practices and pray a blessed prayer and rejoice in our Beloved."[i]

There is a kind of dying that occurs when we undergo pain and suffering, but in this suffering a kind of compassion can be learned. "Our dying is sorrowful: but in all this the sweet eye of kindness and love never leaves us, nor does the working of compassion cease."[ii] We learn things in the *via negativa* that we don't learn anywhere else. Compassion is one of them.

When I was in a serious car accident in the summer of 1976, my knees and back were damaged and became super sensitive. For two years I was in pain for twenty-four hours a day. I refused to take pain pills, because I wanted to learn what pain had to teach me. I continued to accept speaking engagements, and I would fly to gigs, but every step on the terrazzo floor at O'Hare International was excruciatingly painful—and the distances to planes was longer than I ever remembered when my body was well. In the process of choosing to go *into the pain*, however, I learned some significant lessons. Among them was that one can endure a lot of pain, but the energy it takes distracts from doing many other things. Another lesson learned was about the real meaning of compassion and of the specialness of Mother Earth, for the difference between walking with my wounded knees at O'Hare and walking on Mother Earth was the difference between night and day. I became so grateful to Earth for her softness that absorbed my pain and did not add to it. Yet the earth remains firm in its own way.

Julian offers some blunt advice about dealing with pain when she says: "It is God's will that we do all in our power to keep ourselves strong, for happiness is everlasting and pain is passing and will end." All pain comes to an end, she advises. "Therefore it is not God's will that we pine and

---

[i] S 101.
[ii] D 80.

mourn over feelings of pain, but that we get better and continue to enjoy life."[i] She resists all temptations to victimhood. She advises us to "take our trials and dis-eases as lightly as we can. For the more lightly we take them and the less price we set on them, for love, the less pain we will have in feeling them and the more thanks and refreshment we will have for them."[ii]

Julian also talks candidly about meditating on the pain and suffering that Jesus underwent at the hands of the Roman Empire. After all, her visions occurred at the time of Good Friday, the commemoration of his torturous death on a cross. That death, of course, was a political act not unlike lynching, one that was meant by its very cruelty to alert all citizens to the ignoble punishment due anyone who dares to challenge the empire.

About Jesus's "dark night" Julian writes: "The divinity leapt from the Father into the womb of the maiden, descending into form to take on our human nature, and in this descent he was mortally wounded. His wounds are our own flesh, in which he was to experience unbearable anguish and fatal suffering."[iii] She makes explicit that she is not just talking about Jesus, but about all of us who suffer in the flesh. Nor is she thinking of just individuals who are Christians, but about the whole of humanity when she says, "Christ himself embodies all humanity."[iv] Jesus suffered "all the pains associated with the human condition, and [God] did not spare him from any suffering."[v] He did not escape "the conditions of misery" that many humans undergo.

She presents a vivid picture of Christ dying on the cross. "As I watched him dying, the words of Christ came to my mind, 'I am thirsty.' At that moment, I perceived in him a double thirst: one physical, the other spiritual. . . . The physical thirst was caused by the lack of moisture, when all his blood was drained and his blessed flesh and bones were left all alone without wetness of any kind. Abandoned, the blessed flesh was dying drying, the nails twisting in the wounds." She continues her graphic impression of his condition as she saw that "the cruel hardness of the huge nails, driven deep into the tenderness of his sweet hands and feet, combined

---

[i] D 42.

[ii] D 112.

[iii] S 139.

[iv] S 139.

[v] S 140.

with the weight of his blessed body, made the wounds grow wider and the flesh began to sag from hanging there for so long. The garland of thorns bit into his head parched with dried blood, binding and chafing him. . . . The continual pressure of the thorns created gaping wounds in his head." The result? "I was filled with sorrow and fear."[i]

The first thing we must learn from this vision is the bluntness and directness with which she faces Jesus's—and, correspondingly, *our*—suffering. She is teaching us not to sentimentalize, cover over, or (like many politicians) go into denial about the suffering we are undergoing as we face both the coronavirus and climate change. We should not run from the sorrow, fear, and grief, but we should *stay connected* to our feelings. Only the truth will make us free, and we must confront that truth directly. James Baldwin put it this way: "Not everything faced can be changed, but nothing can be changed until it is faced."

Do not run from the bad news, she is saying. Do not seek refuge in addictions that cover over the facts and numb our feelings and eventually our capacity to respond creatively and effectively. Do not let a refuge in bad habits distract us from the realities at hand. Assist those who need assistance in whatever ways we can—from wearing masks to burying the dead; from providing food if we can to organizing groups to learn or play over the internet; from serving on the front lines if we are healthcare providers to helping the truth come out if we are journalists; loving and caring for our children and instructing them and caring for our elders and our sick.

The second takeaway here is that Julian is sharing with us her experience of entering into *her own* near-death experience that accompanied her meditations on that of Jesus. It is significant that her books begin with both Jesus's death and her own. Her sickness and near-death seem to have triggered a kind of initiation, even a shamanistic kind of initiating, in which she herself came ever closer to losing everything. Just as Thomas Aquinas teaches that there are "two resurrections," so too did Julian undergo a death and resurrection experience prior to the full complement of visions. To resurrect, one must first die.

In the time of the Black Death in the Middle Ages, a common practice was to wear the bird masks that symbolized the black bird of prey—the

---

[i] S 42–43.

presence of death. A pandemic, whether in the fourteenth century or the twenty-first century, renders us familiar with the death all around us. Julian also underwent a profound initiation into death when she became an anchoress, locked away in a cell to "leave the world behind." She had already experienced a dying to the world, as she learned to live through a permanent "sheltering in place."

Julian was not unfamiliar with death, and that is what bequeathed her such a rich resurrection that she describes in her Showings. This sets her apart from so many of her contemporaries, who barely recognized the resurrection at all. The first resurrection, Aquinas assures us, is about waking up in this lifetime. Julian did that. But first, like Jesus, she had to die. There are genuine lessons here for us as we participate in our own dances with death. There is no resurrection sans death. Such a death may be a kind of annihilation of our previous lives or work or identities or selves. It can even be simply a death to what we once called "the normal."

Moving Beyond Denial and Addiction

When we find ourselves in pain and a time of uncertainty and loss, we are easily prone to numb the pain, and "painkillers" are everywhere in our culture. Consider the hundreds of thousands of Americans who have died from opioids pushed by "big pharma" corporations and the complicit doctors that have devastated so many communities in contemporary America. Julian, like Hildegard and Aquinas before her, reminds us to live life with passion. What follows from living with passion is to expect delight but be prepared for hurt. "Mirth and mourning," as Julian reminds us, are both realities that touch us at the root. Stay open to both.

Psychologist Anne Wilson Schaef, in her book *When Society Becomes an Addict*, warns us that addiction is invariably about numbing ourselves to pain. She writes that an addiction "keeps us unaware of what is going on inside us. We do not have to deal with our anger, pain, depression confusion, or even our joy and love, because we do not feel them or we feel them only vaguely."

The mystics insist that we not numb ourselves to pain—or to joy—but rather enter deeply into both, that we become genuinely familiar with "what is going on inside us." That is surely Julian's message. Both the *via negativa* and the *via positiva* are real—in fact, they are the most real things in our lives. So enter both fully.

Schaef warns us that addiction can take over social structures, families, and groups of people as well as individuals when she cautions how "in time, this lack of internal awareness deadens our internal process, which in turn allows us to remain addicted." Addictions can kill us. If we do not conquer the addiction the result is death. "We will die. This dying process does not happen at only a personal level: it is also systemic to our culture." It will poison the systems that create our institutions—it will bleed into all our professions and institutions from education to law, from politics to economics, from religion to journalism. It is deadly.[2]

One addiction that requires attention is that of *denial itself.* I was amazed, while participating in a 2017 conference on climate change in Orlando, to learn that the governor of Florida, who resides in the northern panhandle, had sent out a decree that no state employee could use the word "climate change" in any official state correspondence—while, in southern Miami, there were several inches of water on the sidewalks because the seas are rising! The power of the human imagination to live with our heads in the sand is proof of our vast powers of imagination—and self-deception.

The same pattern repeats itself when it comes to the coronavirus, where some politicians are telling citizens it does not matter whether you wear masks, that it will "all disappear," that we can just ride out the virus and pretend it isn't killing hundreds of thousands of people and permanently debilitating still more. Our powers of self-deception should not be underestimated. Our immense minds can be put to the use of truth-seeking and healing—or to the use of denying and hiding from the truth. That is why Meister Eckhart can say that "God is the denial of denial." If God is truth, then to deny denial is to allow the truth to flow. In a time of pandemic that strategy is quite literally a matter of life and death.

Julian urges us to move beyond addiction and fear of pain or suffering—and surely beyond denial. She is not afraid to dwell on the shadow, the darkness that accompanies a pandemic. She invites us to do the same. She assures us that we are stronger than we think and that we can endure much that life asks of us.

She obviously did not dwell inordinately on the grief of suffering and loss in her time, though she was living through a pandemic much more lethal than ours and with far fewer remedies. Her *Showings* faces darkness and suffering directly—but it does not dwell there.

Far, far more of her revelations and instructions are aimed at *remedies* for the dark night we undergo than is the attention she pays to the plague itself (which in fact she never once mentions by name). While not denying the darkness, neither is she dwelling on it. There is a deep lesson here for us also. While acknowledging the wounded world in which we live, do not dwell exclusively on the wounds. Instead, follow Julian who dwells on the remedies, the medicine.

Companions in the Dark Night

Julian is not alone in undergoing the dark night of the soul. Mechtild of Magdeburg (1210–80) underwent her dark nights and names them for us. As a Beguine she was often under suspicion and attack, and so she often had to move from place to place. The Beguines, being neither nuns in a cloistered convent (which is where all nuns were ensconced at the time) nor married women, did not fit easily into a society that wanted women "in their proper place." Indeed, Pope John XXII, who condemned Meister Eckhart only a week after his death, also condemned the Beguines seventeen times! (Which, of course, more or less indicates that his condemnations were not sticking.)

The animus coming from men in places of power toward Beguines did not make life easy for these women, who were committed to create for themselves an alternative lifestyle and ministry of service to the poor, the young, and the sick. They earned their own living, often through sewing, making stained glass, and knitting, while they lived in often modest-sized communities. Their enemies were clearly very threatened by them and often made up libelous stories of their being "loose women" because they were neither married nor behind cloister walls. In other words, they could not be easily controlled (a perennial issue for patriarchy).

One Beguine, Marguerite Porete, was burned at the stake in Paris in 1310 for a book she wrote called *Mirror of the Simple, Annihilated Souls and for Those that Tarry Solely in Desiring and Demanding Love.* Witnesses report that she refused to recant when inquisitors demanded it, and that when they brought her into the public square to be burned she stayed upright and strong to the end. I have written elsewhere of how Meister Eckhart worked closely with the Beguines and, in fact, seems to have kept Porete's ideas alive by incorporating them into his own sermons.[3]

Mechtild suffered her share of calumny and abuse. In her journal, which she published as *The Flowing Light of the Godhead*, she talks of much joy and rapture, play and purpose, work for justice and compassion. But she also shares poignantly her experience of the dark night in entries like the following: "There comes a time when both body and soul enter into such a vast darkness that one loses light and consciousness and knows nothing more of God's intimacy." How deep is this darkness? "At such a time, when the light in the lantern burns out, the beauty of the lantern can no longer be seen." We can easily forget the light and the beauty and even the lantern itself. What do we learn at such times? "With longing and distress we are reminded of our nothingness." It is a time for learning, for seeing anew our smallness in the grand scheme of things and in the vast world.

How should one respond? Mechtild turns to prayer: "At such a time I pray to God: 'Lord, this burden is too heavy for me!' And God replies: 'I will take this burden first and clasp it close to myself and that way you may more easily bear it.'" So she does not sit on her pain, go into denial, or run from it by numbing herself with addictions. Instead, she lets it out by complaining to God—and she finds that divinity itself takes on her suffering. This, after all, is what the Christ story tells us, and it parallels vividly the manner in which Julian meditates on the suffering of Jesus on the cross.

Yet Mechtild's suffering is not resolved; the dark night continues. "But still I feel that I can bear no longer the wounds God has given me, unanointed and unbound. My enemies surround me. O Lord, how long must I remain here on earth in this mortal body as a target at which people throw stones and shoot and assail my honor with their evil cunning?" The attacks keep coming, and she begins looking forward to the escape that death might bring. She is at the end of her rope.

The telling of her inner suffering goes on: "I am hunted, captured, bound, wounded so terribly that I can never be healed." She tastes despair; she is near the bottom and feeling abandoned by God. "God has wounded me close unto death. If God leaves me unanointed I could never recover. Even if all the hills flowed with healing oils, and all the waters contained healing powers, and all the flowers and all the trees dripped with healing ointments, still, I could never recover."[4]

Mechtild longs for relief and finds some in the story of Jesus's sufferings. "I am ill and I long deeply for the health-giving draught which Jesus Christ himself drank." Something came of that thirst that Jesus underwent—a fire was tapped into. "He drank of it so deeply that he was on fire with love." God replies to her entreaties in this way: "I wish always to be your physician, bringing healing ointment for all your wounds. If it is I who allow you to be wounded so badly, do you not believe that I will help you most lovingly in the same hours?"[5]

Mechtild shares with us the wisdom she learned from undergoing dark nights when she writes: "From suffering I have learned this: That whoever is sore wounded by love will never be made whole unless she embrace the very same love which wounded her."[6] The lesson seems twofold: first, don't run from the pain or diminish its deepness; and, second, embrace the pain, burn the dualism between suffering and joy, the *via negativa* and the *via positiva*. Life demands both.

She also instructs us how to embrace nothingness and turn it to service of others (consider how Alcoholics Anonymous does this for its members with great success). "Love the nothing, flee the self. Stand alone. Seek help from no one. Let your being be quiet. Be free from the bondage of all things. Free those who are bound. Give exhortation to the free. Care for the sick but dwell alone. When you drink the waters of sorrows you shall kindle the fires of love with the match of perseverance—this is the way to dwell in the desert."[7] Yes, we sometimes do dwell in a desert. That is what the dark night of the soul feels like. Pain and feeling yourself in the desert are part of life—and especially if you are trying to do what is right and to serve. "Only one without great guilt or sin suffers pain."[8]

John of the Cross (1542–91) was a sixteenth-century Spanish Carmelite friar who was both mystic and prophet. His parents were disowned by his father's aristocratic family because his father had married a poor woman who was of mixed blood. Racism and classism drove his father to leave home entirely, so he moved in with his poor seamstress wife in a kind of barrio or ghetto. The struggling couple had three sons: one was a dwarf (John), another was mentally handicapped, and a third was healthy. There was much love in the family, however, but John's father died when he was six years old. His mother, practically penniless with three young children in tow, went to her in-laws to beg for some support. They refused her, so John's single mom raised the three children by scraping together a hard-earned living. John knew about strong women.

John managed to get the Jesuits to educate him and then chose to enter the Carmelite Order. Teresa of Ávila picked the newly ordained John of the Cross to attempt to reform the male wing of his order as she was doing with the women. Not surprisingly, the Carmelite men did not respond kindly to his efforts and locked him up in a tiny cell where they tortured him and deprived him of food and water. Losing strength and knowing that he would die soon if he did not escape, he made a dramatic getaway that, had he failed, would have resulted in being captured and most likely beaten to death. He managed to lower himself down sheets tied together on what was, serendipitously, a night with no moon—a dark night. John of the Cross, too, died a death and underwent a first resurrection.

John wrote an iconic poem of that escape from near-death at the hands of his own brothers, which he called, "The Dark Night: Song of the Soul, which Rejoices at Having Reached that Lofty State of Perfection: Union with God by the Way of Spiritual Negation." In his poem he celebrates the darkness that befriended him in his escape.

> Once in the dark night
> when love burned bright with yearning, I arose
> (O windfall of delight!)
> and how I left none knows—
> dead to the world my house in deep repose;
>> in the dark, where all goes right,
> thanks to a secret ladder, other clothes,
> (O windfall of delight!)
> in the dark, enwrapped in those—
> dead to the world my house in deep repose.
>> There in the lucky dark,
> none to observe me, darkness far and wide;
> No other light, no guide
> except for my heart—the fire, the fire inside!
> That led me on

true as the very noon is—truer too!—
to where there waited one
I knew—how well I knew!—
in a place where no one was in view.
O dark of night, my guide!
night dearer than anything all your dawns discover!
O night drawing side to side
the loved and lover—
she that the lover loves, lost in the lover!

The poem, the struggle, comes to a happy ending: the beloved is reunited with his lover. As with Julian, the great darkness calls forth a purification of the soul that can lead to a greater joy and gladness than ever imagined. Delight and repose follow.

I stayed, not minding me;
my forehead on the lover I reclined.
Earth ending, I went free,
Left all my cares behind
among the lilies falling and out of mind.[9]

John celebrates the darkness of the night that allowed for his escape. With no moon, he had no light to guide him. For me, the most significant lines in the poem (this translation is by John Frederick Nims) for our and Julian's time of pandemic are these:

There in the lucky dark,
none to observe me, darkness far and wide;
No other light, no guide
except for my heart—the fire, the fire inside!
That led me on.

In a time of deep darkness, even "lucky darkness," there is little or nothing to steer by but the fire deep in our hearts. John Updike spoke about "sex, stoicism and the stars" as being the one guide we have to go by in modern times. But John and Mechtild and Julian offer another—the fire that is hiding most deeply in our hearts. That is why the dark night can so readily bring out the best in us, that which burns most deeply in our hearts. That "spark of God" (Eckhart) urges us on. To what? Follow it and learn. We will try to do this using Julian as our guide in the following chapters of this book.

In a culture as thoroughly marinated in instant gratification and consumer fetishes as ours, one so deeply in bed with consumer capitalism and instructed daily in how best to worship the gods of the latest gadgets that promise to make life easier and quicker and more satisfying—but never accomplishes delight and repose—the experience of the dark night is a deep wake up call. Whether it comes at us from climate change or coronavirus or failures of politicians or the destruction of ideals of democracy or failures of religious promises, or personal pain or combinations thereof, there is plenty to grieve, and there is much dust to be tasted. Loss is in the air, as the dark night knocks loudly on the doors of our souls. Julian dared the dark night; like Mechtild and John of the Cross, she even prayed for it to awaken her. She did not run from it, but rather hung around to learn what it had to teach her. It can do the same for us.

2

GOODNESS, JOY, AWE

God is all that is good. . . . God says "I am the sovereign goodness of all things." —Julian

The specific death that Julian experiences in her vision was that of Jesus, and she presents his suffering in considerable detail. But her showings went beyond that of death (the *via negativa*) to what matters most: goodness, joy, and awe (the *via positiva*). She spends years—decades, even—turning over her experiences and visions in her head and heart. And she lives a long life in service to others by her work as a counselor and spiritual director to many, both in person and, of course, through all three versions of her book. In the process, she becomes a healer for others, mirroring the motherly, compassionate dimension to divinity that she writes about so convincingly. She births light into a world ravaged by darkness and anxiety, and she instructs us in doing the same.

As much as Julian speaks directly to deep pain and suffering and invokes the experience of Jesus on the cross as an archetype of such pain, she spends far more time teaching us to pay attention to experiences of joy and goodness and awe. Why? She tells us that Goodness "is the quality of God that meets evil with good."[i] For her, retrieving and remembering goodness and recovering a sense of goodness, is at the heart of combatting suffering and evil.

Julian advises us that when it is hard to see the goodness of things,

---

[i] S 163.

when one is mired in the darkness and chaos is everywhere, it is *all the more important* to remember the goodness of things. Derek Walcott, a Caribbean poet who won the 1992 Nobel Prize in Literature, declared in his acceptance speech that "the fate of poetry is to fall in love with the world *in spite of history.*" To fall in love is to acknowledge goodness; goodness is about love, and love is about goodness. The goodness we must acknowledge in a time of pandemic and of human malfeasance is the goodness of nature itself and existence itself. It is deeper than history; far deeper than journalism, it reaches down to being itself. Julian knew this. Neither a sentimental nor even a personalistic love is needed in times like ours so much as *a love of creation*, a metaphysical love—which is to say, a love of being itself.

What a complete counterpoint Julian's theology is to that of the flagellants who responded to the plague by traveling from town to town whipping themselves for their sins, which they surmised were the cause of the pandemic! They called for *more* suffering and hatred of self and body because of guilt over sin. Julian's response, however, is the complete opposite. As we will see in subsequent chapters, she urges a love of the body and has trouble entertaining thoughts about sins at all. She urges people to abandon ideas about a God who judges and punishes people, says God has no wrath, and instead counsels people to dwell on goodness, joy and awe.

For Julian, the remedy for making it through hard times is to remember *that* we are here, *why* we are here, and *what a privilege it is* to be part of the vast beauty and goodness of existence. I believe if she knew what we now know about our presence in this amazing universe, which has journeyed for 13.8 billion years and has expanded to include two trillion galaxies (and is still expanding), she could not have been even more overjoyed. She encourages us to live as fully, joyfully, and gratefully as possible. This is what Meister Eckhart meant, after all, when he proclaimed that "if the only prayer you say in your whole life is 'thank you,' that would suffice." And this is what Thomas Aquinas meant when he said that true "religion is supreme thankfulness or gratitude."

All this is what mystics call the *via positiva*, and Julian is no stranger to this way. In fact, the deep experience of the *via positiva* is her primary medicine for living a life of wisdom in the midst of a pandemic. Let us hear her out.

A Metaphysics of Goodness

"God had revealed his goodness with such abundance and plenitude," observes Julian.[i] We live in a world abundant and overflowing with goodness—and "the first good thing is the goodness of nature."[ii] Here she tells us to get out of our own stuckness with the human condition and open our eyes and hearts to the abundant goodness found in nature. The sky, the stars, the moon, the waters, the earth, the trees, the flowers, the animals, the birds, the whales, the elephants, the dog or cat who is our companion, the rivers and the forests—are they not all goodness incarnate? The late monk Thomas Merton used to say that "every non-two-legged creature is a saint." If he is correct, then there are already very many saints in the world all around us. There is a holiness to the goodness of things. Indeed, the Cosmic Christ—or if we prefer, the Buddha Nature—shines forth from all beings.

Julian warns us that our "faulty reason" can often, and especially when times are rough, render us "too blind to comprehend the wondrous wisdom of God, too limited to grasp the power and goodness" of what is being revealed to us.[iii] We must open up both our minds and hearts to recognize what is really around us, how much goodness surrounds us, and how much beauty. She calls us to recognize what she saw early in her vision—namely, that "life is short,"[iv] and we should drink deeply of its goodness while we can.

Indeed, Julian identifies divinity with goodness itself when she declares that "God is all that is good. God has created all that is made. God loves all that he has created. And so anyone who, in loving God, loves all his fellow creatures loves all that is. All those who are on the spiritual path contain the whole of creation, and the Creator."[v] Why is that? "God is the same thing as nature."[vi] Julian is echoing twentieth-century poet Bill Everson (also known as Brother Antoninus), who says "most people experience God

---

[i] S 84.

[ii] S 156.

[iii] S 77.

[iv] S 22.

[v] S 23.

[vi] S 171.

in nature or experience God not at all." Julian calls God "the very essence of nature"—she is speaking of all of nature including human nature. Grace and nature for her "are all aspects of a single goodness, and where one operates, all are operating within us."[i]

It is God who will "refill what is lacking and restore us with the action of mercy and grace, which will abundantly pour into us from his own natural goodness." Thus goodness is natural to God. "This natural goodness stimulates the flow of mercy and grace, and also the natural goodness that he has given us enable us to receive the action of mercy and grace."[ii] We possess a "natural goodness" and "our essence" lies in the Holy Spirit who is "God-All-Goodness."[iii] Thus goodness surrounds us in the manifestation of all of nature but it also flows through us on a regular basis; it is Spirit at work in and through us.

Julian is urging us to wake up to the goodness all around us, within us, and embedded in our work. To wake up to goodness is to wake up to God's presence. Goodness lies deep in the foundation of things; being itself is good, existence itself is good—indeed *very good* as Genesis one puts it. The first chapter of Genesis lays out the unfolding of creation, including humanity, which comes late but comes as part of the "very good" cosmos.

Julian is so keen on a sense of goodness that one might say she is building a *metaphysics of goodness.* Creation is good, and it speaks to us of both its goodness and our own—provided we open our hearts and minds to hear that wisdom. If we are dwelling in self-pity or guilt or focusing too much on suffering, we miss these deeper lessons of living. It is as if Julian took Thomas Aquinas's teaching—which he repeats often—about "original goodness" and runs with it, building her whole worldview on it. Hers is thoroughly an "original blessing" theology (more on this term below).

Julian expounds richly on the beauty of human nature this way: "Of all the natures [God] created, it is in human nature that he placed complete wholeness, power, beauty, goodness, majesty, nobility, reverence, preciousness, and honor."[iv] One might question whether human nature

---

[i] S 155.

[ii] S 157.

[iii] S 162.

[iv] S 171.

and history have lived up to this accolade, but one thing that cannot be questioned is how thoroughly convinced Julian is of our potential as humans. Deep down in humanity she observes an underlying goodness, and in this passage she calls us forward to our "better selves" and harnessing our "better angels" to make good things happen.

Julian elaborates on what it means to say God is goodness when she declares that the divine love "flows from the natural goodness of God." Furthermore, "God is natural in his very being. That is to say, the goodness in nature is God. He is the ground, he is the essence, he is the same thing as nature."[i] To say that the goodness in nature is God is to urge us to find the goodness in nature and to spend time with it. To meditate on it, to let it speak to us heart to heart. Meditation is not just letting go of thoughts, however. It can also mean that we steer our thoughts to the goodness and beauty of nature within and around us. Dwelling on goodness is dwelling on God; it is to put oneself in the presence of God.

This emphasis on God as goodness and goodness as God is so stark in Julian that it offers her primary medicine for surviving a time of struggle and chaos. She urges us not to deny the suffering on the one hand, but on the other to focus more on the goodness found deep within life and nature. After all, isn't the threat to life so frightening precisely because we cherish the goodness of life?

In many respects Julian echoes the teaching of Meister Eckhart when he asks: "Who is a good person? A good person praises good people." Eckhart is dealing with this same experience that is so foundational to his (and Aquinas's and Julian's) view of the world. Together, they are urging us to "Look for goodness! Seek it out. Be a hunter-gatherer after goodness. And that itself will demonstrate your own goodness." In that teaching, as in Julian's, we are reminded that we sometimes must go out of our way to find goodness; life is not always easy or evidently positive. We need a spiritual path that is one of praise. As the Rainer Maria Rilke put it, "walk your walk of lament on a path of praise." Praise is a response to goodness; praise and goodness are bigger than fear and sorrow, thus we can wrap lamentation and sorrow into something beautiful, and this love of goodness keeps us going.

Eckhart also, by calling us to praise good people, is addressing that

---

[i] S 171.

vice we call envy. Envy recognizes goodness but wants to shoot it down, make war with it, compete with it to the point of snuffing it out in another. To choose praise instead of competition is itself a sign of goodness. Julian would very much approve.

Julian recognizes what she calls God's "unending goodness" whereby the "supreme goodness of God" plays out on a daily basis. His is an "endless goodness" that seeks to protect us. Indeed, God reveals the Godself to Julian in these words, "I am the sovereign goodness of all things."[i] Mercy itself "is an action that comes from the goodness of God."[ii]

Awakening to Joy

Julian turns ecstatic when she lays out what she calls the "five supreme joys" of God. In emphasizing the joy of divinity, she seems to be echoing the words of Thomas Aquinas, who says that "sheer joy is God's and this demands companionship." Thus all creation, including the human, is a celebration. It exists to render God joyful, and it exists because God was so joyful that divinity demanded company with whom to share the joy.

During a recent radio interview about my most recent book on Aquinas, the interviewer confessed: "I was raised Catholic but I left the church because of the constant message I was getting about suffering and the cross and the crucifix everywhere. But when I saw Aquinas teaching that 'sheer joy is God's' and that 'joy is the human's nobles act,' I have to ask you: Isn't this a revolution in religion?" Yes, it *is* a revolution in what many people have understood religion to be about for hundreds of years. Indeed, it turns a patriarchal and pessimistic version of religion inside out and upside down. Aquinas, Eckhart, Julian, and the entire creation spirituality tradition present a religious vision that is a far cry from the sinned-based religious consciousness preaching a punitive father god and where guilt, shame, and punishment come wrapped in an ideology of original sin. Starting religion with original goodness and original blessing—and, therefore, with the cosmos—moves away from patriarchal pessimism in its myriad manifestations. It invites far different responses. It gets us out of our collective narcissism as a species.

---

[i] D 104.

[ii] S 85.

Julian names the five supreme delights of divinity this way: "God rejoices that he is our Father. God rejoices that he is our Mother. God rejoices that he is our Beloved and we are his true lover. Christ rejoices that he is our Brother. Jesus rejoices that he is our Savior." These are five supreme joys in which divinity cannot cease being joyful, and "Christ wants us to rejoice in them, too, and praise him, thanking and loving and endlessly blessing him."[i] No wonder she says, "Jesus is true, lasting joy" who possesses a "loving face" that invites each of us to reconnect our "outer and inner" faces so that joy shines forth from us.[ii] She recognizes three faces in Jesus—one is suffering, yet "glad and joyful," another was of "empathy and compassion," but "the joyful face was shown more than the other two and continued the longest."[iii]

The divine joy calls us to our own capacity for joy. Julian calls us to the *via positiva* and our capacity for rejoicing, praise, thanks, love, blessing. She insists that "the fullness of joy is our birthright"—and it goes along "with intense yearning and unshakable trust."[iv] For Julian, we are born into a *"birthright of never-ending joy."* She writes: "We will not take possession of our birthright of never-ending joy until we find ourselves fully gratified with God and all his actions and judgments, loving and nonviolent toward ourselves and toward all our fellow seekers and able to love everything God loves."[v] There are guideposts to tapping into that birthright, including responding gratified with all that life offers us, the "well and the woe" therefore; learning to love oneself and be nonviolent toward ourselves and others; and loving all of creation as God loves all of creation. Here she is adapting Jesus's teaching to "love others as oneself." Healthy self-love is what we project onto others and into our relationships with others—and notice that the "others" are *all of creation*—that is, "everything God loves." These are the means to recognizing joy and staying in it no matter what circumstances we endure.

One need not be a genius to recognize how great a distance Julian is, theologically speaking, from sixteenth-century theologians like John

---

[i] S 142.

[ii] D 116.

[iii] D 117.

[iv] S 104.

[v] S 122.

Calvin, who declared that life is a curse and "totally wretched" and humans are "nothing but filth inside and out" and subject to a "horrible despair." Or Martin Luther, who said that the world is the "devil's kingdom" and "all bad" and humans should "despair totally of themselves in order to be able to receive Christ's grace."[1] Pessimism goes hand in hand with patriarchy. Julian leaves pessimism in the dust.

For Julian, once we dwell on goodness in creation it affects our view of the world and fills us with joy. "To behold God in all things is to live in complete joy."[i] The "all things" of which she speaks includes difficult and trying things. Eckhart says that "everything praises God. Darkness, privations, defects, evil too praise God and bless God."[2] Julian says that our joy can be "complete" when we find God in all things. Meister Eckhart said the same when he declared that the sign that we have undergone breakthrough is that we see God in all things.

We cannot sit idly by while suffering happens to ourselves or others; we must dig deeper to find the treasure that lies hidden within life and within ourselves. Julian urges us to become gardeners of the soul as well as the soil when she says: "There is a treasure in the earth that is a food tasty and pleasing to the Lord. Be a gardener, dig and ditch, toil and sweat, and turn the earth upside down and seek the deepness and water the plants in time. Continue this labor and make sweet floods to run and noble and abundant fruits to spring." In this thrilling teaching Julian returns us to the joy of working in and with nature, the outer work becomes the inner work and the inner the outer. Indeed, this work of gardening is not only a holy inner work with the soil and with the soul, but it becomes our worship as well. "Take this food and drink and carry it to God as your true worship."[ii]

Divinity, as Julian sees it, turns a happy face toward us even when there is hardship. "The blessed face that our Beloved turns toward us is a happy one—joyous and sweet. He sees us lost in love-longing, and he wants to see a smile on our souls, because our delight is his reward." Compassion is part of the exchange with the divine. As is delight.[iii]

We learn from the story of Jesus that joy, not suffering, is the basic dynamic of life. Says Jesus to Julian: "Now all my bitter pain and cruel

---

[i] S 84.

[ii] D 84.

[iii] S 192.

labor have been transformed into endless joy and bliss for me and for you." We are entwined in a mutual joy for "your pleasure is my pleasure. Your endless delight in me brings me unending delight." It all comes from love, for joy derives from love. "Oh, how I have loved you!" exclaims Jesus. Such a revelation renders "us all exceedingly happy."[i]

The mutuality of shared joy multiples, for "God wants us to rejoice with him in our liberation." He also "wants our souls to be completely and joyfully engaged. For we are his bliss, and he delights in us and wishes for us to delight in him, with his grace." It is because "we are liberated," that "Christ endlessly rejoices."[ii] From Julian's perspective, joy even "permeates the passion" of Christ because its purpose—our liberation—was its goal. She dares talk about "the joy and bliss of the passion."[iii] We can translate this for living through a time of pandemic by understanding that, within the larger context of things, all can work to a greater purpose. Good things can happen when we learn lessons of letting go, reevaluating our structures and values, and living fully.

One way to grasp a spiritual concept is to consider its opposite. What constitutes the opposite of joy? I would venture to say *acedia*. Acedia is dullness and boredom and apathy; it is often translated as sloth, but that is too narrow an understanding. Thomas Aquinas defined it as "the lack of energy to begin new things" and "a sadness about divine things." Thus depression and despair and passivity and boredom and what I call *couchpotatoitis* are also expressions of acedia, along with what Hildegard of Bingen calls "indifference," or not caring. She decries how the soul can becomes "weakened by the coldness of indifference and neglect," but also how the soul can be re-fired and made strong "to all manner of good by the fire of the Holy Spirit."[3] For her, acedia includes dullness born of boredom, sloth, uselessness, and a "numbness" that "postpones doing good" and lacks the vigor to fight for justice. Acedia prevents one from accomplishing the greatness of one's work. One refuses to live *and work* fully.

Joy, then, is the oppose of acedia—joy at spiritual things that awaken fire. For joy is the fruit of love. A joyless person or culture is one starving

---

[i] S 60.

[ii] S 56f.

[iii] S 56.

for love and out of touch with the love of the universe and earth all around us.

In discoursing at length about joy, Julian is calling us away from acedia and toward joy. She is lighting the fire of joy in us. In fact, Julian invented the word *enjoy* in English which draws from "rejoicing" (*enjoier* in old French).[4] Aquinas teaches that acedia "tears charity out by its roots" and that it derives from "sadness" and Julian's medicine to sadness and acedia is joy.[5]

Remembering Awe

Julian instructs us to take delight and joy in life and to respond "with reverence and humility." Awe has something to do with encountering greatness, something which is bigger than ourselves—the sacred. Holiness and awe go together. Here is how Julian puts it: "The reverence I speak of is holy awe, which is entwined with humility. The creature sees the Divine as wondrously great and the self as wondrously small. This is a virtue instilled in all God's loved ones."[i] Rabbi Heschel says that "awe is the mind encountering the universe." This awareness of awe and greatness can be a regular thing. Eckhart says that for the person who is awake, breakthrough does not happen once a year, once a month, or even once a day—but *many* times each and every day.

Julian says that "we experience this gift when we feel the Presence of God"—it is a yearning deep within us, and it is holy. "This holy awe is the experience we most deeply long for because it creates a wonderful sense of security, true faith, and certain hope. The greatness of love makes this awe sweet and delicious."[ii] From this tasting of holy awe a sense of security, faith and hope emerge. Love is its source, as in the case of joy that we considered above. Goodness is the object of love, love and goodness, like joy and awe, travel side by side with goodness. The *via positiva* is here for the taking.

Julian names both the reality of the *via positiva* and *via negativa*, as well as the tension between them, when she tells us that "two duties belong to our souls. One is to reverently marvel. The other is humbly to endure,

---

[i] S 179.
[ii] S 179.

always taking pleasure in God."[i] To "marvel reverently" is to admit awe into our lives. Awe is marveling. Indeed, the root meaning of "miracle" is *marvel*. Marveling is a holy act, and we should indulge ourselves often in marveling. As Eckhart says, "isness is God." And as Julian says, "goodness is God." There is a lot of isness and goodness, beauty and wonder, in the world. We need to immerse ourselves in it on a regular basis—and especially when suffering and chaos are all about us.

Awe is a kind of fear or dread—Aquinas calls awe a "chaste fear" and the only fear that we should allow into our hearts. I remember when I was living for a few months during the winter at Marshfield, Massachusetts, which is located on the ocean. At the first winter storm, I went near the beach to watch the immense waves and feel what was happening. But soon I realized I had to stand by the side of a house and hold on to it to peer out at the ocean—it was so wild and so demanding I would have been sucked into the waves had I just stood on my own. That was awe. And it was scary. But a reverent, holy, and chaste awe it was. A sacred moment transpired, and it has kept itself alive in my memory for fifty years.

Julian pictures awe this way, that there will come a time when "all creatures will be filled with such wonder and amazement, their reverent awe surpassing any they have ever felt before, that the pillars of heaven itself will vibrate and quake." But "there will be no pain in this fear and trembling. Rather, this is the proper response to the absolute majesty of the Divine when his creatures behold him. We tremble and quake with the abundance of joy that fills us, marveling at the greatness of God, our Creator, and lost in wonderment in the face of the smallest thing he has created. Such a sight fills all creatures with wondrous humility and quietude." Notice that even the smallest thing in creation brings wonderment to us and invites us to get lost in contemplating it. Realizing the greatness of divinity, we are moved to a "reverent awe [which] is the proper response to the supreme beauty of the Divine."[ii] The supreme beauty of the divine hunts us out daily.

Julian names the fear or dread that is built into awe. "Love and dread are siblings. . . . They are rooted in us by the Goodness of our Creator, and they will never be taken away." Notice again how primal *goodness* is

---

[i] S 116.
[ii] S 204.

to Julian's understand of creation and Creator. Indeed, Meister Eckhart says that "whenever we talk about God the Creator we are talking about goodness." This is exactly Julian's understanding also. Julian continues: "Love is in our nature, and we are given the grace to adore God. Dread is in our nature, and we are given the grace to feel awe. God's grandeur and majesty inspire awe." Again, awe is about being in the presence of something very great and vast. The universe is awesome for sure.

Like Aquinas, she dismisses fear that is not the holy fear of awe. "All fears other than reverent awe are not real and the most dangerous ones are those that come disguised as holiness. Holy awe produces "natural fruits . . . through the grace-giving action of the Holy Spirit." Holy awe "drives us into the arms of the Mother" where we recognize the "everlasting Goodness of God."[i]

Julian recognizes that love and awe, like love and goodness, go together. "God's Goodness evokes love. It is our nature as his servants to revere God in awe, and it is in our nature as his children to adore him for his goodness. Although holy awe cannot be separated from love, still they are two different things. . . . You cannot have one without the other."

Julian holds thoughts about awe that anticipate some of the deep insights from Rabbi Abraham Joshua Heschel in the twentieth century. For Heschel, "awe is the beginning of wisdom" and thus awe plays a prominent place in our quest not just for knowledge but for wisdom—a quest Julian also celebrates. In addition, Heschel has this to say about awe: "Wonder, radical amazement, the state of maladjustment to words and notions, is a prerequisite for an authentic awareness of that which is."[6] Julian seems to bring this sense of wonder to the table in spades—as did her ancestors, Hildegard, Aquinas, and Eckhart. Awe is so stunning to our system and our consciousness, proposes Heschel, that we become "shocked at the inadequacy of our awe, at the weakness of our shock." Heschel warns us of what happens when we lose our sense of awe. "Forfeit your sense of awe, let your conceit diminish your ability to revere, and the universe becomes a marketplace for you."[7] It is telling that both Heschel and Julian talk about the intrinsic relationship of "awe" and "reverence." Awe gives birth to reverence, but consumerism and capitalism can abort awe.

A brain researcher at Stanford University approached me several years

---

[i] S 201.

ago following a lecture and said to me that, after twenty years of studying the brain, he had come to the conclusion that "the right hemisphere is all about awe." I equate the right hemisphere with the intuitive brain—our *mystical* brain, if you will. Einstein equates mysticism with "standing rapt in awe" and says that it is from our intuition that we derive our values—not from the rational brain. It follows, then, that a society or educational system that diminishes awe also diminishes a sense of values.

Rachel Carson (1907–64) recognized that our powers of awe begin in childhood, and she lamented how readily adults put it behind them. "A child's world is fresh and new and beautiful, full of wonder and excitement. . . . For most of us that clear-eyed vision, that true instinct for what is beautiful and awe-inspiring is dimmed and even lost before we reach adulthood." Her number one wish for children? "A sense of wonder so indestructible that it would last throughout life, as an unfailing antidote against the boredom and disenchantments of later years, the sterile preoccupation with things that are artificial, the alienation from the sources of our strength."[8] Maybe this is what Jesus had in mind, too, when he said to a group of adults that they must become like children if they are to receive the reign of God.

With Rabbi Heschel, Einstein, and Rachel Carson—as well as Hildegard, Aquinas, and Eckhart—on the subject of awe, Julian finds herself in very good company. She urges us to join in and to put awe, along with goodness and joy, fully into our consciousness and our longing. Where does this longing come from? "This holy longing springs from God's love and is balanced by humility, submission and patience which are also divine virtues he has endowed us with."[i] It is a holy longing that derives from the love of God.

The *via positiva* receives a hearty practice from Julian; indeed, she endorses it as the grounding that sees us through the darkness of times of pandemic and other dark nights of soul, society, and species. It is the medicine that gives us strength to carry on; it reunites us to the Source.

---

[i] S 139.

A Coda for Thanksgiving

In this chapter we have been naming the deep acts of goodness, joy, and awe—the *via positiva*—as the medicine to combat the distress and despair that pandemics and other hard times can elicit. Thomas Aquinas alerts us to how despair, while not being the worst way of missing the mark, is nevertheless the "most dangerous." When we are in despair we cannot act, we lose interest in ourselves and others. Despair kills the soul and kills compassion. Thus we must work to follow the *via positiva* and our powers of goodness, joy, and awe. The sum result of the *via positiva* is a recovery of reverence and gratitude for existence—no matter the suffering involved. Struggle and unknowing cleanse our souls so that we learn not to take for granted.

Julian, like Aquinas and Eckhart before her, also invokes gratitude or thankfulness as the bottom line of spirituality when she writes: "This is the holiest prayer—the loving prayer of thanksgiving in his sight."[i] There is no substitute for thanksgiving or gratitude. While the *via positiva* provides the medicine in hard times, sometimes we must stretch our memories to recall those gifts that we may forget under stress—such as the gift of existence itself, life itself, breathing, seeing, hearing, and all the ways of being-with in this world of wonder and surprise and possibilities.

Julian elaborates on the role of thanksgiving in our spiritual life when she writes: "Giving thanks is also part of prayer. Thanksgiving is a true, inner awareness. Charged with the quality of reverence and loving awe, we turn ourselves with all our might toward the actions our good Lord guides us to, rejoicing and thanking him inwardly. Sometimes the soul is so filled with gratitude that it overflows and breaks into song: 'Good Lord, thanks be to you! Blessed are you, O God, and blessed may you always be.'"[ii] Our loving actions follow. We arise from undergoing goodness, joy, and awe to share it with—and educe it from—others. Shaping a world where all can share in the *via positiva* is good work indeed. It is enough to make us break into song.

---

[i] S 101.
[ii] S 101.

3

NATURE AND GOD ARE ONE

God is the same thing as nature.—Julian

Many in Europe in the fourteenth century, so traumatized by the plague that attacked indiscriminatingly and came repeatedly in waves, began to curse nature. Nature was to blame. "Every time I go into nature I withdraw from God" uttered the too well-known theologian Thomas à Kempis (1380–1471).

Julian would have none of this denigration of nature, even though she lived through the pandemic from the age of seven until she died in her eighties. For her, nature was a place of grace, and human nature nested in the arms of a holy nature.

For Julian, one reason for honoring and not cursing nature is this: "God rejoices in his creation and creation rejoices in God. They are endlessly marvelous to each other. In the act of marveling, we behold our God—our Beloved, our Maker—utterly exalted."[i] Julian exhorts us to do what she does—*to marvel at nature.* This clearly echoes her teaching in the previous chapter about the importance of awe and wonder. We rejoice and marvel at creation. But she is also pointing out something amazing—that God, too, marvels at creation—indeed, "they are endlessly marvelous to each other." Awe is mutual between Creator and creation. Indeed, we become "stilled by holy awe" and this stillness takes us over.[ii]

---

[i] S 109f.
[ii] S 107.

The Goodness and Grace of Nature

Julian believes that "reason, mercy, and grace operate in harmony to bring us all good things, the first of which is the goodness of nature."[i] The goodness of nature is not something "out there" but is inside of us, nature penetrates us in all its goodness. We are in it and it is in us. So goodness is in nature and in us and we in it. And nature precedes all other blessings, all other experiences of goodness. It is *first*.

Today's science instructs us that matter is "frozen light" or very slow moving light. Julian, of course, was not aware of today's science, but she did share a similar appreciation for light—and applied it to her dark times of pandemic: "This light is carefully measured out and available to us when we need it in the depths of the night. This light is the source of our life, and the night is the cause of our pain and woe." When suffering befalls us, we must be willing to "acknowledge and believe in our light, and we walk wisely and powerfully in it."[ii] The *via negativa* and the dark night call for light to return. Light penetrates darkness and redeems it because "I saw that our faith is our light in the darkness of night, and that light is God, our endless day."[iii] It is telling that she talks of "*our* light" in both of these observations—she is very much personalizing light—it is not just "out there," it is within us, it is intimate to us, we carry it about with us. The light is in our bodies, but it is also in our hearts and attitudes. Or at least it *can* be. Julian equates the light with the Trinity: "This light is God, our Father-Mother, our Creator, and the Holy Spirit, inside Christ Jesus, our Liberator."[iv]

God's nature includes Life, Love, and Light. "In Life is the astonishing familiarity of home. In Love is courtesy as befits a relationship. And in Light is endless Nature-hood." Endless naturehood—what a rich way of talking about the richness of nature and indeed of evolution if we might use a term more familiar to us than to Julian. Evolution is a kind of "endless naturehood" and divinity dwells within it.[v] If matter is frozen

---

[i] S 156.

[ii] S 220.

[iii] S 221.

[iv] S 221.

[v] D 131.

light and light is interchangeable with matter, then Julian is speaking to twenty-first-century science when she calls light "end-less Naturehood."

She elaborates on her understanding of "naturehood" when she declares that "God is the Ground, the Substance, the same thing that is Naturehood. God is the true Father and Mother of Nature and all natures that are made to flow out of God to work the divine will shall be restored and brought again into God by the liberation of persons through the working of grace."[i] "Endless naturehood" includes endless friendship, for "in God is endless friendship, space, life and being."[ii]

Julian rejects the dualism between nature and grace found in thinkers like Augustine and Thomas à Kempis in favor of a great mingling of both. She writes: "Nature and Grace are in harmony with each other. For Grace is God as Nature is God. God is two in manner of working and one in love. Neither Nature nor Grace works without the other. They may never be separated."[iii] Thus the divine penetrates all of us and all of creation and this is grace. For "nature is all good and beautiful in itself."[iv] Where humans have degraded nature, the incarnation makes it graceful again. Indeed, "grace was sent out to liberate nature and destroy sin and bring beautiful nature once again to the blessed point from whence it came: that is, God." Nature itself becomes purified in the process. "Nature has been evaluated in the fire of trying experiences and no flaw or fault has been found in it."[v] In this way, "all the blessed children who come out of God by Nature will be returned into God by Grace."[vi] Indeed, "our being is nature," and we build on nature to compassion and then to grace.[vii]

What a call she makes in these passages for us to honor nature once again! If only we would cease ignoring and harming nature, as has happened so efficiently in the industrial revolution that is our inheritance. If divinity can take on nature and dwell among it, Julian insists, then surely

---

[i] D 106.
[ii] D 82.
[iii] D 108.
[iv] D 109.
[v] D 109.
[vi] D 111.
[vii] D 102.

humans, so eager to connect to the divine, can roll up their sleeves and do what is necessary to preserve the goodness and beauty of nature.

Love, Joy, and Nature

Perhaps it is due to her deep experience of the omnipresence of the divine and grace in nature that Julian can exclaim: "The fullness of joy is to behold God in everything!"[i] For "God is the same thing as Nature."

Julian believes that "when it comes to knowledge of love, it is here that we are most blind. . . . It is our ignorance of love that causes all the trouble." Even though love is embedded within nature and God is "all-love," we have a hard time believing that. "The notion that God is All-Love and wants to do everything? There we stop." What follows is fear and failure. "This ignorance is the greatest obstacle for God's lovers, in my opinion. . . . A certain fear persists, and it continues to hinder us."[ii] Love and fear are not compatible; so often we prefer fear to love. It is a choice we make—but an *ignorant* one in Julian's view of things.

Humans and all creatures are made for love, and love goes way back in our existence and that of the cosmos that birthed us. "I saw that God never *began* to love us. For just as we will be in everlasting joy (all God's creation is destined for this), so also we have *always* been in God's foreknowledge, known and loved from without beginning."[iii] Joy and love go together and both extend to all of creation, humans "have been given creation for our enjoyment because we are loved."[iv] Of course, we are expected to love creation back and work to keep it healthy and happy also.

Panentheism

Panentheism is another way of talking about the relationship of divinity and nature—it literally means *everything is in God* and *God is in everything*. Sixty years before Julian, Mechtild of Magdeburg exclaimed, "The day of my spiritual awakening was the day I saw all things in God and God in all

---

[i] D 60.

[ii] S 198.

[iii] D 88.

[iv] D 72.

things."[1] In other words, her coming to the awareness of panentheism was a breakthrough in her spiritual maturity. Julian reports similar awakenings and calls it the cause of mirth or joy in her when she writes, "It is a matter of mirth that our Beloved, our Creator lives inside us and that we live in him. This is because of his great goodness and faithfulness in which he keeps us safe."[i] This mutual indwelling includes the sharing of the divine goodness that we discussed in the previous chapter. Our joy and mirth derives from the Creator living in us and we living in the Creator—here we arrive at the experience of panentheism.

Indeed, for Julian, the experience of panentheism is the very meaning of faith: "Faith is nothing else but a right understanding of our being—trusting and allowing things to be: A right understanding that we are in God and God whom we do not see is in us."[ii] God is within but we do not see God—air is within and we do not see that either. But its effects are known. "In my understanding I saw God in a point. In seeing this I saw that God is in all things. God works in creatures because God is in the mid-point of everything and does all that is done."[iii] God as center, as midpoint, is that our experience too?

To experience and to remember panentheism results in joy and rejoicing. It is rich medicine for dark nights. "We would be right to rejoice that God dwells within our own souls, and even more so that our souls dwell in God. Our soul was created to be God's dwelling place, and he who is uncreated is also the place where we dwell. It is a sublime realization to see with our inner eyes that God, our Creator, dwells inside us, and it is an even more exalted thing to understand inwardly that the essence of our soul, which is created, dwells in God."[iv] What a profound lesson of panentheism, how we and God dwell within one another, that Julian is teaching us here!

Her understanding of her experience of panentheism brings her to this striking awareness: "I saw no difference between the divine substance and the human substance; it was all God. I was able to accept that our essence is in God, that our essence is a creation of God, and that God is simply

---

[i] S 195.
[ii] D 89.
[iii] D 37.
[iv] S 149.

God."[i] It follows that because "our soul is oned to God, unchangeable goodness, and therefore between God and our soul there is neither wrath nor forgiveness *because there is no between*."[ii] It is hard to get more non-dualistic than this.

To know oneself is to know God and to know God is to know oneself. We undergo a *longing* that "compels us to find our own soul where it is, which is in God." We learn about self and God together, for "whether we are moved to seek God or our own souls, the Holy Spirit leads us through grace to know them both as one. Both impulses are good and true."[iii] To discover self is to discover God, and to discover God is to discover self. This parallels the teaching by Meister Eckhart that "all the names we give to God come from an understanding of ourselves." An invitation exists, therefore, to pursue self-discovery and God discovery. "Both by nature and grace, we are rightfully endowed with the yearning to know ourselves with all our might. In the fulfillment of this knowledge, we shall come to clearly and truly know our God in the fullness of never-ending joy."[iv] A never-ending joy accompanies those who have worked to know themselves better, to examine our shadow and our wounds as well as our gifts and inner light, to know oneself "with all one's might." Such knowing is demanding.

A deep journey of *inness* takes place with God because "we are enclosed in him, and he is enclosed in us." He calls us inwards, where "he dwells within us in infinite bliss, drawing us ever deeper inward. . . . Our true essence is one with God."[v] Between God and creation there is no between—that is the message of panentheism, as well as the message of the Cosmic Christ, the Buddha Nature, and *tselem*, the image of God that Judaism preaches. Such an understanding offers a re-affirmation of the sacredness inherent in all beings.

---

[i] S 149.

[ii] D 77.

[iii] S 154.

[iv] S 113.

[v] S 159.

The Cosmic Christ

Julian tasted deeply of the cosmos and its meaning as a whole and she shares that with us in her celebrated vision of a hazelnut.

> God showed me in my palm a little thing round as a ball about the size of a hazelnut. I looked at it with the eye of my understanding and asked myself: "What is this thing?" And I was answered: "It is everything that is created." I wondered how it could survive, since it seemed so little it could suddenly disintegrate into nothing. The answer came: "It endures and ever will endure, because God loves it." And so everything has being because of God's love.[i]

A wonderful vision of the oneness of things! And also the fragility of our existence. I am reminded of the Voyager 1 journey through space and out of our galaxy and how, on looking back, it took a photo of its journey. What we see is a number of brightly lit points. Scientists point to one and say, "This is earth." Our earth is fragile and special sitting so alone, a pinpoint of light in the deep realms of space. It is easy to feel for it what Julian felt for the hazelnut in her hand.

Shortly before Julian was born, Meister Eckhart also called on the hazelnut to teach a deep spiritual lesson, saying that we are "seeds" of God and "a pear seed grows into a pear tree, a hazel seed into a hazel tree, and a seed of God into God."[2]

Julian looks on Christ often, as all creation mystics do, as the Cosmic Christ—that is to say, the divine presence in all things. John's gospel talks about Christ as the "light of the world" and the "light in all beings," or the divine *logos* that resides in all things. The Cosmic Christ arises often in Julian's awareness, as when she tells us that "in God's sight, all humanity is one person, and all people are a single humanity."[ii] There is a universality in Christ "who embodies all humanity" for he "represents the spiritual yearning in us all. Christ is all spiritual seekers and all spiritual seekers are Christ."[iii]

---

[i] D 25.
[ii] S 133.
[iii] S 139.

And "God makes no distinction between the blessed Christ and the least soul among us."[i] Here she is surely referencing the story of Matthew 25, in which Jesus proclaims: "Do it to the least of these, and you do it to me."

The "I am" sayings found in John's gospel are sayings of the Cosmic Christ created by gospel writers who lived after the historical Jesus. Jesus did not speak those "I am" sayings so much as the Christ did, which is to say the community that lived after Jesus who, interestingly, did not hesitate to put words into Jesus's mouth. Among these "I am" statements are "I am the light of the world"; "I am the good shepherd"; "I am the resurrection and the life"; "I am the living bread"; and so on. In our book, *The Stations of the Cosmic Christ,* Bishop Marc Andrus and I teamed up with two artists to present the deep meaning and application of the Cosmic Christ archetype. These artists, M. C. Richards and Ullrrich Javier Lemus, rendered the "I am" sayings and other rich images and stories of the Cosmic Christ found in the gospels such as the nativity, baptism of Jesus, transfiguration, Matthew 25, the crucifixion, resurrection, ascension, and Pentecost.[3]

In *The Coming of the Cosmic Christ,* I share many significant passages of scripture that refer to the experience of the Cosmic Christ. New Testament scholar Bruce Chilton reminds us that Paul, the first author in the Christian Bible, actually writes about a *metacosmic Christ!* A Cosmic Christ is also found in an early Christian text we know as the *Gospel of Thomas,* which was written about the time of Paul's letters. Clearly, therefore, the archetype of the Cosmic Christ is present at the very launching of the Christian movements.[4] Strange indeed that it got covered over and almost lost from the time of the Black Death to the twentieth century. *But Julian did not abandon it.*

The Celtic tradition boasts many rich "I am" poems, and very likely Julian, living in England, was aware of that tradition. The following Celtic poem is very ancient—Celtic bard John O'Donohue called it "the first poem ever composed in Ireland." It goes as follows:

> I am the wind which breathes upon the sea,
> I am the wave of the ocean,
> I am the murmur of the billows,
> I am the ox of the seven combats,

---

[i] S 149.

I am the vulture upon the rocks,
I am a beam of the sun,
I am the fairest of plants.
I am the wild boar in valour,
I am the salmon in the water,
I am a lake in the plain,
I am a world of knowledge,
I am the point of the lance of battle,
I am the God who created the fire in the head."[5]

Creating "I am" poems is a powerful practice by which to integrate the Christ in us and in nature with our daily experiences.

Julian creates her own "I am" poems. Here is one:
Our Lord Jesus oftentimes said:
"This I am,
This I am.
I am what you love.
I am what you enjoy.
I am what you serve.
I am what you long for.
I am what you desire.
I am what you intend.
I am all that is."[i]

Here we have a profound statement on the presence of the divine within all things—in this case within all the layers of human consciousness. Our hearts are richly named here—love, joy, service, longing, desire, intention—the Christ is in all of it. And finally, an ultimate statement on the Cosmic Christ, "I am all that is." The Cosmic Christ is the Christ in all things, the divine light in all things.

Julian lays out another "I am" poem naming the divine:
God said: "This I am—the capability and goodness of the Fatherhood.

---

[i] D 47.

This I am—the wisdom of the Motherhood.
This I am—the light and the grace that is all love.
This I am—the Trinity.
This I am—the Unity.
I am the sovereign goodness of all things.
I am what makes you love.
I am what makes you long and desire.
This I am—the endless fulfilling of all desires."[i]

Julian turns an "I am" motif into an "I do" motive as well, since we are to operate from our being after all. Being and action go together for Julian, just as Eckhart indicated when he advised us to worry less about what you should do and more about who you are. For if your being is good your works will be good, and if your being is just your works will be just.[6] Says Julian: "See! I am God. See! I am in everything. See! I never lift my hands off my works, nor will I ever. See! I lead everything toward the purpose I ordained it to from without beginning by the same Power, Wisdom and Love by which I created it. How could anything be amiss?"[ii]

Everything has a purpose, Julian is saying; and that purpose comes to fruition in its activity—and surely this includes humanity itself and all our human activities. Heart and action merge—Julian urges us to put our awe to work: "Have holy awe and humble love, in our heart and in our actions."[iii] Holy awe is to make its way into the world by way of our actions.

Julian displays a very real grasp of the Cosmic Christ when she describes the crucifixion in a cosmic context: "All creatures of God's creation that can suffer pain suffered with him." Even the cosmos was affected, "the sky and the earth failed at the time of Christ's dying because he too was part of nature."[iv] Notice that it was Christ's relationship to nature that brought about the suffering of nature at his death. Julian does not succumb to a sentimental or a privatized notion of Christ's death, but recognizes it as a tragedy that the entire creation participated in. In this regard, she is in tune with the gospels themselves, which lay out many stories of how the whole

---

[i] D 104.
[ii] D 39.
[iii] S 202.
[iv] D 44.

of nature responded to Christ's death—stories that include the eclipse of the sun, an earthquake with the dead leaving their tombs, the veil of the temple rent in two (and one of those veils we now know pictured the universe), all of this apocalyptic imagery telling of a great catastrophe that affects all of creation. A *cosmic* event; a *Cosmic Christ* event.[7] The Jewish tradition tells us that the whole universe stands on two pillars of justice and righteousness, and when injustice happens those pillars are broken and the whole earth is in trouble. Thus, the apocalyptic imagery of the crucifixion.

Julian picks up on that imagery and avoids an overly personalizing interpretation of it—such as the notion that we killed Christ by our sins (we were not part of the Roman Empire of 2000 years ago, after all)—though we are part of empires today that are killing rainforests and oceans and countless species, thus crucifying the Christ all over again. We engage in the killing of the Christ when we engage in the killing of others who are all "other Christs." Those others may be other human beings or generations to come of species of animals, birds, bees, finned ones. Standing by while global warming happens is killing the Christ. Ecocide is a form of killing Christ. This is what it means to recognize—as Julian does—that "Christ too was part of nature."

In a time of the culmination of the ravaging of nature that has been motivating our species for centuries, and especially from the industrial revolution to today, it is a question of our very survival—and that of countless other species—that we hear with clear hearts and minds how sacred Julian sees the earth and nature. Thomas Berry has warned that "we will not save what we do not love, [but] it is also true that we will neither love nor save what we do not experience as sacred."[8]

4

THE DIVINE FEMININE AND THE MOTHERHOOD OF GOD

God feels great delight to be our mother.—Julian

No theologian up to the late twentieth century has so devoted herself or himself in an explicit way to the return of the divine feminine than has Julian of Norwich. Her preferred manner of doing so is to speak often and develop an understanding of the *motherhood of God* and also the *motherhood of Christ.* She also speaks of the motherhood of the Trinity and invokes Mary, the mother of Jesus, as an exemplar of divine motherhood.

In invoking the divine feminine, Julian is of course informing us about how we need a balanced sense of gender to survive and even thrive in a time of pandemic and after a pandemic has left us.

Poet and essayist Adrienne Rich, in her iconic study, *Of Woman Born: Motherhood as Experience and Institution,* has much to say about motherhood, its light, and its shadow. I found it deeply instructive to return to while writing about Julian of Norwich's understanding of divine motherhood. Rich begins her book this way:

> All human life on the planet is born of woman. The one unifying, incontrovertible experience shared by all women and men is that months-long period we spend unfolding inside a woman's body. . . . Most of us first know both

love and disappointment, power and tenderness, in the person of a woman.

There is much to suggest that the male mind has always been haunted by the force of the idea of *dependence on a woman for life itself,* the son's constant effort to assimilate, compensate for or deny the fact that he is "of woman born." Motherhood is earned, first through an intense physical and psychic rite of passage—pregnancy and childbirth—then through learning to nurture, which does not come by instinct.

Most women have been mothers in the sense of tenders and carers for the young. . . . It is with a woman's hands, eyes, body, voice, that we associate our primal sensations, our earliest social experience.[1]

Rich also equates motherhood with "the powerful Goddess."[2]

Earlier Champions of the Divine Feminine

Julian is not alone among medieval mystics in calling forth the divine feminine and/or the motherhood of God. Sixty-five years earlier, Mechtild of Magdeburg declared that "God is more than a father" and expressed her commitment to the motherhood of God this way: "God is not only fatherly. God is also mother who lifts her loved child from the ground to her knee."[3] As we saw above, Mecthild, like Julian, is an overt panentheist. Mechtild connects her panentheism to maternal imagery of embracing and surrounding when she writes: "The Trinity is like a mother's cloak wherein the child finds a home and lays its head on the maternal breast."

One hundred years before Mechtild, Hildegard of Bingen (1098–1181) tells us that "divinity is …like a wheel, a circle, a whole, that can neither be understood, nor divided, nor begun, nor ended."[4] She speaks of our relationship to the divine as something round and compassionate when she tells us we are "surrounded with the roundness of divine compassion."[5]

For good reason do I call Hildegard, in my most recent book about her, *Hildegard of Bingen: A Saint for Our Times,* a "herald of the divine feminine," and I point out the irony of her being declared both a saint and a doctor of the church by the anti-feminist papacy of Benedict XVI, because Hildegard's life work ushers in a prodigious sense of the divine feminine. Indeed, I suggest that she is a Trojan horse in the otherwise patriarchal Vatican, and lurking in that horse are all kinds of codes for the divine feminine.[6]

Hildegard says we are "hugged" and "encircled by the mystery of God"—more imagery of roundedness. She says, "God is as round as a wheel." She offers panentheistic imagery when she declares that "Just as a circle embraces all that is within it, so does the God-head embrace all." The circle of creation is all encompassing. "Now here is the image of the power of God: This firmament is an all-encompassing circle. No one can say where this wheel begins or ends." She describes the Creator as "carrying" creation as a mother carries her infant in the womb, "God carries us forever in the divine providence and does not forget us."[7] The divine love is an unforgetting love, as is that of a mother.

Hildegard recognizes Mary as a cosmic figure and indeed an archetype of the divine feminine when she calls her the "ground of all being." Again, "You have established life! Ask for us life. Ask for us radiant joy. Ask for us the sweet, delicious ecstasy that is forever yours." For Hildegard, Mary is "Mother of all joy, ground of all being, a glowing, most green, verdant sprout."[8]

Hildegard develops the important image of Wisdom, which is feminine in the Bible and indeed around the world. For Hildegard, she is maker of all that is. She describes encountering a young woman in a powerful vision:

> I heard a voice speaking to me: "The young woman whom you see is Love. She has her tent in eternity. . . . It was love which was the source of this creation in the beginning when God said: 'Let it be!' And it was. . . . The young woman is radiant in such a clear, lightning-like brilliance of countenance that you can't fully look at her. . . . She holds the sun and moon in her right hand and embraces them tenderly. . . . The whole of creation calls this maiden 'lady.' For it was from her that all of creation proceeded, since Love was the first. She made everything. . . . Love was in eternity and brought forth, in the beginning of

all holiness, all creatures without any admixture of evil.
Adam and Eve as well were produced by love from the
pure nature of the Earth.[9]

This stunning vision underscores the Creator as a woman and Love as the
source of all creation, earth and humans as well.

Hildegard scholar Barbara Newman says that Hildegard recognizes
"motherhood as theophany. Woman's primary significance in the divine
scheme of things is to reveal the hidden God by giving him birth. In the
meantime, she gives birth to this image in every child that she bears."[10]
Meister Eckhart develops the imperative to give birth also—"the essence
of God is birthing,"[11] he declares and he insists that we are all meant
to be mothers of God. God is feminine, "What does God do all day
long?" he asks. "God lies on a maternity bed giving birth." Furthermore,
when humans give birth, we give birth to nothing less than the Christ.
"What good is it to me, if Mary gave birth to the son of God 1400 years
ago and I don't give birth to the son of God in my person and time
and culture?"[12] Like Hildegard, who talks of a "flowering orchard" that
humans accomplish by our work, Eckhart also honors our creativity and
work as a God-like giving to the world, a birthing of the Christ into history.

On Motherhood in Julian's Time

Brendan Doyle points out in his fine introduction to *Meditations with
Julian of Norwich* the likelihood that the Black Death had a significant
impact on motherhood and mothering in Julian's time. Barbara Tuchman,
in her classic work on the fourteenth century, *A Distant Mirror,* reveals
that "women appear rarely as mothers" in the art of Julian's time. Even
the Virgin Mary is portrayed with the child Jesus always at a distance. No
attempt was made to illustrate a close relationship between mother and
child.

Tuchman's explanation for this phenomenon is tied to the fact that
the survival rate for children was very low in the time of the pandemic—
one out of three. Mothers were, therefore, afraid to come too close to
their children in order to spare themselves the agony of almost certain
separation. Doyle poses the question: "Is Julian also trying to redeem the

word 'mother?'" It is very likely that Julian had a wonderful childhood and a very special mother. Doyle sees Julian's emphasis on authentic mothering in a time of mother distancing as "another prophetic counterpoint to the culture of Julian's time," that and Julian's continued sense of joy and trust in nature.[i]

By writing at length and in depth about the nature of mothering, clearly Julian is standing up to the *Zeitgeist* of her time that so minimized the role of the mother. She digs deep to keep that primal relationship alive and present in everyone's sight.

Julian on the Divine Feminine and the Motherhood of God

We have seen previously some of Julian's teachings about the motherhood of God, but she abounds with still more. Consider the following statements. "Just as God is truly our Father, so also is God truly our Mother."[ii] Joy and parenting go together in divinity: "God feels great delight to be our Father and God feels great delight to be our Mother."[iii]

What are the characteristics of a mother for Julian? Compassion is one such characteristic. "Compassion is a kind and gentle property that belongs to the Motherhood in tender grace." What is this tender compassion about? "Compassion protects, increases our sensitivity, gives life and heals."[iv] At the root of compassion lies love in action. "The ground of compassion is love and the working of compassion keeps us in love." Compassion, then, is love at work. It is an action. "Compassion is a sweet gracious working in love, mingled with abundant kindness; for compassion works at taking care of us and makes all things become good."[v] Compassion is about putting kindness and caring into action. It is our work.

Often the test of compassion is not when things are going well, but when darkness descends and troubles occur. The dark night of the soul invites compassion and stretches our capacity for compassion—it becomes a school for compassion. Failure happens. As Julian puts it, "Compassion

---

[i] D 19.

[ii] D 103.

[iii] D 85.

[iv] D 81.

[v] D 80.

allows us to fail measurably and in as much as we fail, in so much we fall; and in so much as we fall, in so much we die; for we must die if we fail to see and feel God who is our life." Again, as we saw in chapter 1, Julian addresses death and the many deaths we undergo in life, especially during a pandemic. Only after these dyings do we undergo that awakening we know as the "first resurrection."

"Our failing is fearful, our falling is shameful and our dying is sorrowful: but in all this the sweet eye of kindness and love never leaves us, nor does the working of compassion cease."[i] So compassion sees us through falling and failing, fearing and dying. Compassion persists in the hardest of times. It is strong, it is our strength.

The word compassion in both Hebrew and Arabic comes from the word for *womb*. A special bond obtains between the mother and the fetus in the womb, one of profound interdependence. Thus, motherhood and compassion are often connected. Indeed, the basis of compassion is interdependence. This is one reason we might expect an explosion of compassion in our postmodern world, for interdependence, rather than rugged independence, is our current understanding of how the world works (and it is an ancient understanding with the mystics of old, Julian included). Might compassion be another word for *doing non-dualism, for practicing it?*

The strength dimension of compassion can also be called *justice.* This is the biblical meaning of compassion, when we realize, as Eckhart put it, that "compassion means justice." Thomas Aquinas was keen on the link between justice and compassion when he wrote: "God is justice; God is compassion. . . . We find these two things, compassion and justice, in all the works of God. . . . Compassion without justice is the mother of weakness. And therefore it is necessary that they be joined together according to Proverbs 3:3: 'Compassion and truth will not forsake you.'"[13] Justice is that side of compassion that prevents it from being coopted by sentimentalism or feeling run rampant with no sense of the balance that is needed and is integral to deep healing. Anne Douglas, in her classic work, *The Feminization of American Culture,* defines sentimentalism as "rancid political consciousness," a worldview turned in on oneself and one's private feelings and completely lacking in a sense of justice-making. Douglas

---

[i] D 80.

demonstrates how deeply sentimentalism lurked in the modern media beginning with the nineteenth century and surely continuing to today.[14]

Does Julian see the connection between justice and compassion that Eckhart and Aquinas saw? Yes, she does. "God wants to be known and loved through Justice and Compassion now and forever," she writes. Indeed, "Justice is that thing that is so good that it cannot be better than it is." Like Eckhart and Aquinas before her, Julian states bluntly that "God is Justice." And "God creates Justice in all who will be liberated through goodness."[i]

Another characteristic of mothering for Julian is service. "A mother's service is nearest, readiest and surest," she tells us. And such ready and sure service belongs in a unique way to divinity. "This office no one person has the ability or knows how to or ever will do fully but God alone."[ii] God is the ultimate mother. A mother serves and often all day long and into the night when a child is sick, scared, or in need. God the Mother does the same.

Our role when God is serving us is to receive and respond with the trust of a child. "It is natural for the child not to despair of the mother's love. It is natural for the child not to be overconfident. It is natural for the child to love the mother and each brother and sister."[iii] Julian recognizes our childlikeness as an exalted state. "I understand no higher state in this life than childhood with its minimum of ability and skill unto the time that our gracious Mother has led us to our Father's joy."[iv] She seems to be taking quite literally Jesus's teaching that "until you become as a child, you will not receive the kingdom/queendom of God." She invites us to entertain the child within, treating it with care and respect and a readiness for child-like spontaneity.

There is an "expanding and saturating action of the Mother," as Julian sees it, that carries us to the Source. "The motherhood of mercy and grace brings us back to our source, where we were created by the motherhood of love. This mother-love never leaves us."[v] A motherhood of love created

---

[i] D 61.
[ii] D 105.
[iii] D 110.
[iv] D 110.
[v] S 165.

us. Here we see echoes of the vision of Hildegard that we saw above, that Lady Love made all things.

The Divine Motherhood of Jesus and the Christ

Julian acclaims the divine feminine and divine motherhood not only in God the Creator but also in Jesus and the Christ. Julian often speaks about the motherhood of Jesus and the motherly qualities of Jesus. In doing so, she underscores the importance of incorporating the divine feminine into our entire mindset, including our understanding of the Christ. For example, she assures us that Jesus "is our Mother, Brother and Liberator."[i] In the light of faith, she teaches, "our Mother, Christ, and our good Lord, the Holy Spirit, lead us in this passing life."[ii]

Again, "Jesus is our true Mother in whom we are endlessly carried and out of whom we will never come."[iii] Here we have what I have come to call "christological panentheism." Like all panentheism it is rounded, it is about embracing, and here she is speaking of our dwelling in the divine womb, a place of great serenity and interconnectedness. Consider this other naming of a Christological panentheism, our being "in Christ" (a term that St. Paul used so frequently in his epistles that biblical scholar John Dominic Crossan says "you can hardly keep count"—thus clearly a very ancient term found in the earliest Christian sources.[15] "The high Goodness of the Trinity is Christ in whom we are all enclosed and he in us."[iv]

There is a message here that addresses profoundly the "original wound" named by the psychologist Otto Rank, who maintains that we all possess an original wound of separation from our mothers that haunts us all our life. This trauma is triggered by the many separations we undergo in journeying through life. In Julian's teachings, we find an explicit mention of healing that deep wound, just as Rank predicted when he said that only the *unio mystica* provides the deep healing we all need. Such a oneing comes by way of love and art, he believes.

Julian comes close to repeating herself when she says, "Our savior is

---

[i] D 101.

[ii] D 132.

[iii] D 99.

[iv] D 90.

our true Mother in whom we are endlessly born and from who we shall never be separated. . . . We are enclosed in him and he is enclosed in us." Panentheism indeed!

She discourses on what goes on when Christ dwells in us. "He dwells within us in infinite bliss, drawing us ever deeper inward. He wants us to be his helpers in this inner work" and we are to give him "all our attention."[i] Thus we are to be coworkers with him and Spirit undergoing the work together. Julian saw in her vision that "the Second Person is really our Mother. This beloved being works with us as a parent here on earth. . . . In taking on our flesh, the Second Person became our Mother of Mercy." Christ is a mother of mercy—but what are the consequences of that mothering? "Our Mother keeps all our parts together and works on us in various ways. We profit and grow in Christ-the-Mother. Through her mercy, she restores and redeems us. Through his passion, his dying, and his resurrecting, he makes us one with his own essence."[ii]

Julian endeavors to bring the divine feminine into the tradition both of the Trinity and of Christ himself, not hesitating to name him as a "she," as do so many Christian feminists today. One sees her own womanhood and potential motherhood playing an assertive role in these discourses on Jesus and Christ and God as mother. She credits Christ, "our Mother of Mercy," with "reconciling and transforming us into the perfect human being."[iii]

Julian ascribes the source of all motherhood to "Christ Jesus" who "is our true Mother. He is the source of all motherhood, and we have our being for him, protected by all the sweet love that endlessly accompanies motherhood."[iv] She does not fall into a trap of literalism, however, but continually imagines a variety of ways of considering Jesus and Christ. He is "our Mother, our Brother, and our Redeemer. . . . Jesus is our true Mother in nature. And by taking on our created human nature he is our Mother in grace. All the loving acts and sweet natural tasks of motherhood belong to the Second Person of the Trinity."[v]

Julian recognizes "three ways to look at" the motherhood of God: "the

---

[i] S 159.

[ii] S 161.

[iii] S 162.

[iv] S 163.

[v] S 164.

first is that she created our human nature. The second is that she took our human nature upon herself, which is where the motherhood of grace begins. And the third is motherhood in action." Clearly, she is bringing the divine feminine into the bosom of the Trinity with this teaching. For her the divine feminine is not a *supplement to* divinity but dwells and acts deeply *from within* the entire Godhead. Nature, grace, and action all come together, she says, for it is "All One Love."[i]

Julian recognizes the incarnation, what she calls the "leap of God" into human form and history, to be a deeply motherly act, an act of motherly mercy. "God chose to become our Mother in all ways, humbly and tenderly cultivating the ground of his work in the womb of a maiden. Our transcendent God, the glorious wisdom of the universe, emptied himself into this earthy place and made himself entirely available through our own poor flesh. In this form he himself offered the unconditional service and duties of motherhood."

And what are these duties of motherhood? Julian names three aspects to authentic mothering: "Being nearest to our own nature, the mother's serving is most immediate. Being unconditionally loving, the mother's service is most willing. And being the truest thing there is, the mother's service is most certain. Only God could ever perform such duty."[ii] Mother's work is a godly work, and there is a coworking that takes place between mother and children—one that is immediate, loving unconditionally, and most willing. That relationship is not sentimental for Julian—it is about service, work, and even duty. "Whenever a human mother nurtures her child with all that is beautiful and good, it is God-the-Mother who is acting through her."[iii] Co-creation happens.

A true mother *protects* her child with great tenderness. "This is the nature of motherhood." She adapts her methods and relationships as the child grows, "but her love never changes." And when the child becomes more mature, she "develops his virtues and graces" and chastises his vices.[iv]

---

[i] S 164.

[ii] S 165.

[iii] S 167.

[iv] S 167.

It follows that "our life is grounded in our true Mother, Christ, endlessly guided by his foresight and Wisdom."[i]

The Divine Feminine and the Survival of Our Planet

Since Christ is understood as God's wisdom, we might ask: Is the understanding of Christ as mother related to this notion of Christ as wisdom? Both are feminine. Divine mother, mother of wisdom.

Julian's understanding of the divine feminine permeates her entire grasp of the nature of divinity. She invites us to develop this same mindset. Like other mystics we have seen, she celebrates the embracing that the mother archetype offers. "The deep Wisdom of the Trinity is our Mother. In her we are all enclosed."[ii] Here she is naming Wisdom; and Trinity; and Mother; and being enclosed—four dimensions of the divine feminine named in two short sentences. Building on this grasp of the Trinity, she teaches that "in our coming into being, God All-Power is our natural Father, and God All-Wisdom is our natural Mother, supported by the boundless Love and Goodness of the Holy Spirit. All one God." Love and goodness belong to the Holy Spirit and offer themselves as supporters to the Mother.[iii]

She clearly names the Trinity as feminine when she tells us that she saw "three ways to look at the motherhood of God. The first is that she created our human nature." Here she applies the term "motherhood" and the divine feminine to the Creator, or the first person of the Trinity. "The second is that she took our human nature upon herself, which is where the motherhood of grace begins." Thus, Julian applies the motherly dimension of divinity to Christ. "And the third is motherhood in action, in which she spreads herself throughout all that is, penetrating everything with grace, extending to the fullest length and breath, height and depth. All One Love."[iv] A cosmic vision of the Holy Spirit and of divine love in action for sure. The divine feminine permeates all history and all work.

In ascribing the divine feminine and motherhood and motherly actions

---

[i] S 158, 174.
[ii] D 90.
[iii] S 160.
[iv] S 164.

to the entire Trinity, as she does on many occasions, Julian, in many ways, rewrites Christian theology. She insists on including what Carl Jung called the "fourth side" of the Trinity, the feminine side that has been missing. Thus she introduces a Quarternity as a way to look at divinity. Hildegard of Bingen also had a vision of the Quarternity of the divine in relationship to the human person and painted a picture of it.[16]

In many ways Julian rewrites Christology as well by insisting and repeating often how Jesus and the Christ can be understood as mother and within an archetype of mothering. Jesus offers a profound example of the steadfastness and generosity of a mother's love, having sacrificed and suffered even to the point of death with a "wondrous love." Even then, "he did not want to stop working on our behalf. And so now he must nourish us, which is what a mother does." His nourishment goes on, mother-like.[i] Julian's theology of the sacraments is founded on the motherhood of Christ the Mother.

Julian compares the milk that a mother gives a child to the blessed sacrament that Jesus shares with Christians in the celebration of the Eucharist or Last Supper, the sharing of bread and the wine, "the precious food of true life." In this way, "Christ-the-Mother is entwined with the wholeness of life, which includes all the sacraments, all the virtues of the Word made flesh, all the goodness that Holy Church ordains for our benefit."[ii]

For Julian the word "mother" becomes a special name for the divine— indeed, "this beautiful word 'mother' is so sweet and kind in itself that it cannot be attributed to anyone but God. Only he who is our true Mother and source of all life may rightfully be called by this name. Nature, love, wisdom and knowledge are all attributes of the Mother, which is God."[iii] To be a mother is to be a source of life, and since divinity is the source of *all* life, divinity is preeminently a mother.

The Native American worldview has been described as "aboriginal mother love" by Frederick Turner. If that is so—and it is certainly my experience that it is, with the deep appreciation of "Mother Earth" and "Grandmother and Grandfather Sky" that Native American religion

---

[i] S 166.

[ii] S 166.

[iii] S 166f.

harbors—then Julian is in good company with indigenous wisdom, personified as Pachamama. Once again, premodern wisdom, whether found among indigenous peoples or in medieval mystics, sounds a common note—and a common alarm. When the divine feminine is neglected or ostracized, humanity is in trouble. And Mother Earth suffers, too. Wisdom is banished and its opposite, *folly*, takes over. We seem to be at such a place in history now. The balance between the divine feminine and sacred masculine has been sundered. Climate change and coronavirus emergencies follow. Denial abounds in high places whether it concerns wearing masks in a pandemic or acting decisively on climate change.

Is it a coincidence that it is a teenage girl, Greta Thunberg, who called adults at the United Nations to wake up and address more substantively the onslaught of extinctions engulfing the planet? I don't think Julian would be surprised.

All the more reason, then, to drink in the wisdom of Julian and, of course, the wisdom of the mother who is in all of us. A one-sided patriarchy, complete with empire-building and earth-destruction, has held sway for long enough. The divine feminine is calling us to wholeness. Julian calls us back to a healthy balance—our religions included along with our educational, political, and economic structures. All are out of balance, and therefore all are unjust and unsustainable. The return of the divine feminine is not an option. It is essential for balancing a topsy-turvy world where Mother Earth and women, men, and children are teetering out of control.

Julian makes clear what inviting back the divine feminine does *not* mean for our understanding of divinity. Contrary to many patriarchal images of God as a punitive father and judge, Julian admits to seeing "no kind of vengeance in God, not for a short time, nor for long. . . . In God is endless friendship, space, life and being."[i] Vengeance is in us—we ought to quit projecting it onto Divinity. "I saw wrath and vengeance only on our part. God forgives that in us."[ii] Where does vengeance come from? "A failing of power or of wisdom or of goodness on our part."[iii] Notice the trouble we make for ourselves—and others—when we distance ourselves

---

[i] D 82.
[ii] D 79.
[iii] D 79.

from our goodness, our own power, and our wisdom. We fall into acts of disempowerment, and we exalt a distorted version of divinity—and with it, a distorted version of masculinity and humanity and our own personhood. Folly substitutes for wisdom. Earth suffers. All suffer.

5

TASTING NON-DUALISM

Between God and our soul . . . there is no between.—Julian

The *Shema* prayer is foundational to Judaism. Found in Deuteronomy 6:4, it instructs us that "God is one," or that "oneness is God," or that all things are One and God is One and all things participate together in this oneness. Albert Einstein, a son of Israel, says "This oneness of creation to my sense, is God. This concept of God will unify all nations."[1] In Judaism this awareness of oneness is a primary prayer, and it leads us into the deep oneness that we are capable of entering. And there we find our tasting of the divine.

The Oneing Experience

Julian invented the word *oneing* in English, and even today, seven centuries after she lived, the word is rare for many of us English speakers. Maybe it is time to bring it back and alive again! Other mystics have come up with their own words for the *oneing* experience, words like *ecstasy* and even *getting drunk* (Thomas Aquinas); *breakthrough* (Meister Eckhart); *union with reality* (Underhill); states of insight into depths of truth, illuminations, revelations full of significance and importance (William James); *unio mystica* (Rank); *peak experiences* (Maslow); *flow experiences* (Csikszentmihaly), or *satori* (Buddhism). I, too, have employed *ecstasy*, or what I called "Whee!" in my guide to sensual, prophetic spirituality called *Whee! We, Wee All the Way Home.*

However the terms differ, the exact word is not important—the experience is, after all, beyond words. Mystics invite us to follow up that experience by journeying deep down and into it to taste the charged union with reality and the divine. This is a journey that all mystics undergo—and we are all mystics.

Julian's word for the mystical experience is *oneing*: "In our creation we were knit and oned to God. By this we are kept as luminous and noble as when we were created. By the force of this precious oneing we love, see, praise, thank and endlessly enjoy our Creator."[i] Clearly, Julian identifies our oneing experiences here with our many experiences of the *via positiva*.

She elaborates on the oneing experience of our creation—when did it begin? Our soul "is known and loved from without beginning and in its creation oned to the Creator."[ii] This teaching very much parallels that of Meister Eckhart, who says that we were originally at one in the Godhead—that all things are at one there, and there is no separation. But when we enter the world on emerging from our mother's womb, then we are no longer in sync with the Godhead. We move from the unitive world of the Godhead to the fraught world of creation, history, and God. But when we die, we return to the Godhead and to a unity so perfect that "no one will have missed us" and no one evens asks, "Where have you been?"[2]

How do we undergo the oneing? One way is the way of breakthroughs, ecstasies, and oneings that can occur on a regular basis—Eckhart insists this happens many times each day, in fact. For the person who is awake breakthrough does not happen once a year or once a month or even once a day but "all the time."[3] Furthermore, Eckhart teaches that "in breakthrough I learn that God and I are one."[4] Clearly, he and Julian are on the same page, celebrating God and our "oneing."

Julian tells us "prayer ones the soul to God."[iii] By prayer she would include meditation and contemplation, the prayer of silence and the prayer of chanting psalms or reading them, of creating mantras and chanting them. Prayer also includes the *lectio divina*, whereby one centers oneself with a simple thought or word or insight and lets go of all thoughts to be either in its place or in a place where wisdom can talk to the heart.

---

[i] D 100.

[ii] D 93.

[iii] D 73.

Prayer can also at times mean our talking to God, though more than that it means listening to the divine, which requires what Eckhart called the "inner wealth of an inner silence." One way we "one ourselves to God" is by contemplation, which makes us like the one we contemplate.[i] We also pray when we work for love, justice, and compassion.

Julian tells us that "the fruit and the purpose of prayer is to be oned with and like God in all things."[ii] In other words, she reminds us that all things are already oned to God. Isn't that the meaning of panentheism after all? But we can easily feel distant or out of touch. In its many manifestations, prayer can overcome that distance and let the oneing return. Our *awareness* of the oneing is always going on. Think of our breath—it is oned with us. It is not sometimes here and sometimes not here, but we do not see it (unless it's very cold outside), and we can easily take it for granted.

God is like breath. It is no accident, in fact, that "breath" and "spirit" are the same words not only in biblical languages but in most languages around the world. And one of the creation stories in Genesis tells us that humans were born when God *breathed* the divine breath into clay. God is so close that we cannot see or hear him/her. Sometimes we must redirect our consciousness and focus on that nearness. Aquinas says that God is closer to us than we are to ourselves. And Jesus proclaimed that the "kingdom of God is within you"—and "among you." We must enter the *within* as well as the *among* to taste the kingdom and get the message.

The struggle of a time of pandemic, the kind of darkness and ignorance we discussed in chapter 1, often culminates with a oneing. Letting go and letting be often culminate in a breakthrough. Eckhart teaches that out of nothingness God is born. Despair and suffering, as the late monk Fr. Bede Griffiths taught, often culminates in a kind of "bottoming out" that leads to a breakthrough. Ask members of Alcoholics Anonymous or other groups that journey together into their darkness. Many AA members have told me that they never encountered spirit until they underwent their bottoming out. All grief is that way. When we stay on the path, that path may take us to a better place. This is why Father Bede says that "despair is often a yoga" or a union that takes us to God.

That is what Julian teaches also. In her telling of the crucifixion of

---

[i] S 186.
[ii] D 70.

Jesus she "saw a great oneing between Christ and us because when he was in pain, we were in pain."[i] Suffering is universal; it is common to all of us, and if we face it and do not run from it, it will bring about a great oneing, a great understanding of our common condition as humans. Says Julian: "Those who were Jesus's friends suffered pain because they loved him." It hurts to be with the pain of others, of loved ones. But it also grows the soul.

The Oneing of God and Us

Julian testifies to a "true oneing between the divine and the human, forged in paradise," that makes it "impossible to separate them." When human nature was created, it was "rightfully one-ed with the creator, who is Essential Nature, uncreated—that is, God. This is why there is absolutely nothing separating the Divine soul from the Human Soul." It is love that does this, indeed "in endless love we are held and made whole. In endless love we are led and protected and will never be lost."[ii]

The "humanity of Adam, with all the wounding and weakness that attend the human condition" is everywhere visible. Divinity suffers also since "God shows us that his own Son and Adam are one and the same. We share the strength and goodness come from Christ and also the weakness and blindness that comes from Adam."[iii] Any guilt humans feel is lifted since "Jesus has taken upon himself all guilt. God therefore does not blame us." Christ became a human being "to save all human beings" and "return humanity to a state of grace." In fact, "there is nothing separating divinity from humanity."[iv] And there is nothing separating anyone from Christ since human nature "is so completely entwined with Christ's nature that our true essence can never be separated from his, nor should it be."[v] God sees us as other Christs because "God's love for humanity is so vast that he makes no distinction between the blessed Christ and the least soul among us."[vi]

---

[i] D 44.
[ii] S 147.
[iii] S 137.
[iv] S 138.
[v] S 146.
[vi] S 149.

Oneing is a yearning we all share—and it will come to pass. Indeed, "it is by our longing that we will be liberated. Through our yearning for oneing, we shall come to be one."[i]

Mingling the Via Positiva and Via Negativa

Julian offers additional remedies for facing the facts of the dark night of our species at a time when cover up, forgetfulness, and denial are in the air. The medicines assisted her to endure the Black Death pandemic of her day, as well as the face-to-face encounter with the dying Jesus that motivated the "revelations of divine love" that became her journey.

First, she recognizes and urges us to recognize that life is not all woe—even in the midst of a pandemic. She reminds us that "during our lives here on earth, we experience a wondrous mixture of well and woe. We hold inside us both the glory of the Risen Christ and the misery of the Fallen Adam. Adam's fall has broken us all. We are so fragmented, afflicted in our feelings in so many ways, that we hardly know where to turn for comfort The various pains and transgressions of this life fill our hearts with sorrow and cloud the eyes of our souls."[ii]

Since the eyes of our souls are clouded, we must uncloud them to clarify our perception, so we see life as it is. Yes, there can be plenty of suffering and *via negativa*, but there is also much joy and beauty, awe and wonder, and cause for thanks and gratitude. This is, for Julian, a basic remedy for our troubles in times of the great darkness. She recognizes the omnipresence of goodness beneath all reality and beneath all brokenness, and she identifies Christ as one who "protects us in our dying and, through his gracious touch, uplifts us and reassures us that all will be well" with a sense of shelter.[iii]

She also recognizes the universality of suffering—we all undergo a life experience of "well and woe," of the *via positiva* and the *via negativa*. We must learn to live with and even dance with this dialectic, this tension, and not to dwell to exclusively on one element (joy) or the other (suffering or fear of suffering). Rabbi Zalman Schachter-Shalomi used to say: "There

---

[i] S 139.

[ii] S 142.

[iii] S 142.

is more good than evil in the world—but not by much." This echoes Julian's recognition, too, that "Adam's fall has broken us all," but it does not follow that life contains no joy or delight or meaning. Rather, it is in exploring those other profound dimensions of life that we find medicine to endure—and eventually triumph—over life's woes.

Indeed, for Julian, that is the lesson learned from the Good Friday and Easter Sunday stories. She recognizes there an archetypal reminder of the life/death/resurrection journey that we all make—and that cosmologists today are finding actually makes the world go around and the universe happen. Here is how Julian recalls the story.

> His body lay in its tomb until Easter morning. . . . At this point, all the writhing and wallowing, the moaning and groaning, ended. Our damaged mortal flesh was made whole again. Our Savior turned Adam's old tunic—tight, threadbare, and short—into a gleaming garment—fresh and beautiful, white and bright. He was clothed anew in everlasting purity, more ample and luxurious even richer and lovelier than the clothing I saw the Father wearing! The Father's robes were blue. Christ's clothes were made of light, which blended into a mixture so marvelous that I cannot begin to describe it, for it is composed of pure glory.[i]

"Mirth and Mourning Dance Together"

About this dialectic of joy and sorrow, Julian reminds us that while there is "cause for mirth and cause for mourning,"[ii] the key is to focus and not determine that one moment or feeling is necessarily superior to another. She instructs us to "cultivate our intention and wait for God. We have faith in his mercy and grace, and trust that he is working within us. . . . Sometimes we glimpse more, sometimes we see less, depending on what

---

[i] S 140f.
[ii] S 195.

God gives us the ability to receive. Now he elevates us; now he allows us to come tumbling down."[i] Waiting is part of the journey.

Julian does not pretend that dealing with deep joy or deep darkness is easy—but it is a discipline that we can learn, especially in hard times. "The mixture of sorrow and joy is so powerful that we cannot figure out how to handle it all, let alone assess how our fellow spiritual seekers are doing. The diversity of feelings can be overwhelming." In this passage, ripe with wisdom, she walks her talk, for we sense her wandering along both the *via positiva* and then into the *via negativa* in a back-and-forth process. "In those moments when we sense the presence of God we surrender to him, truly willing to be with him, with all our heart, with all our soul, and with all our strength. This holy assent is all that matters. It eclipses all the wicked inclinations inside us—physical and spiritual—that might lead us to miss the mark."[ii]

But she returns to the reality of darkness and doubt. "Sometimes, however, that sacred sweetness lies deeply buried, and we fall again into blindness, which leads to all kinds of sorrow and tribulation." What to do? Do not "give in to our negative impulses, but draw strength from Christ, who is our defender against all harm. . . . and pray for the time when God will once again reveal himself and fill our hearts with the sweetness of his presence. And so we remain in this muddle all the days of our lives. But our Beloved wants us to trust that he is always with us."[iii]

We find ourselves in a muddle between wellness and woe all our lives, she warns. Get used to it! To live life deeply is to deal with both light and darkness, joy and sorrow. This teaching echoes that of Mechtild of Magdeburg, who says that we are given two wines to drink in this lifetime—the white wine of joy and the red wine of suffering. Until we have drunk deeply of both we have not lived.

Julian offers a parallel teaching when she insists on the marriage of well and woe. Do not run from either; enter both deeply. Do not fall into denial or the temptation of living without passion. Hildegard of Bingen warns us: "O human! Why do you live without passion? Why do you live without blood?" Acedia, or what Julian calls sloth, is the refusal to live life

---

[i] S 142.

[ii] S 143.

[iii] S 143.

with passion, and she considers that one of the worst ways we can miss the mark. Depression, despair, ennui, boredom, and *couchpotatoitis* are today's parlance for acedia—and there is a lot of it going around. Indeed, it has become exacerbated by the apocalyptic warnings coming at us about climate change and the coronavirus.

Christ "delivers us from the misery of earth," Julian says on one occasion—but *only* one occasion.[i] Earth has its miseries, especially during a pandemic. We can only guess at the misery that Julian witnessed first as a child and then throughout her life as the plague kept returning in waves. But the amazing thing is that it is rare that Julian talks about "misery." She indeed speaks about woe, but even then does not dwell on the subject. By her silence she is telling us not to dwell on the misery and woe, but rather to look further behind evil to being and to goodness.

Julian poses the vexing question of how a good God can create a good universe that is ridden with evil. Her response seems to parallel that of Thomas Aquinas, who proposes that when human beings are ignorant "of nature and their place in the cosmos, they may imagine that they are subject to forces that, in fact, they are beyond."[5] He writes: "Sometimes evil is to the good of others or of the whole universe: thus God directs the sin of tyrants to the good of the martyrs."[6] Sometimes evil is relative: a cat dines on a mouse, but the mouse dies. "A mouse is killed by a cat for the preservation of the universe. For this is the order of the universe, that one animal lives from another."[7] A larger context assists somewhat in understanding some evils. Thus, "if all evil were prevented, much good would be absent from the universe. Lions would cease to live, if there were no slaying of animals."[8] Yes, life is violent and messy.

How different is Julian's treatment of "misery" from that of such theologians as John Calvin and Martin Luther, who came two centuries after her and who were quite untouched by a feminist perspective. For them, misery was everywhere, as we saw in chapter 2—and they weren't living through a pandemic like Julian was!

---

[i] S 162.

Beyond Dualisms

Julian resists dualisms. After all, she is a mystic calling us to our own mysticism, our own oneing. While a non-dualist, she is not oblivious that differences exist, and instead of denying those differences or covering them over with sweet talk and sugarcoating, she calls for a mingling. Life demands of us that we necessarily undergo "a wondrous mixture of well and woe,"[i] of light and dark, of *via positiva* and *via negativa*. She assures us that God knows all about this need to mingle, as in fact "God is our true partner in this weaving and joining."[ii] It is a creative and co-creative process, a dance that we weave with the Holy Spirit, a *via creativa* to which we give birth.

Julian calls us frequently to develop our dialectical capacities of seeing the world in a both/and way, instead of either/or. "Whether rising or falling, we are always graciously enfolded in one love. In the sight of God we do not fall and in our own sight we do not stand. While both of these perspectives are true, as I see it, the way God sees is the highest truth." She prefers the glass half-full to the glass half-empty way of seeing the world. She continues: "God's will for us to know the higher truth binds us ever more closely to him. What is most helpful, I realized, is for us to hold both truths together in this life. The higher perspective gives us spiritual solace and true joy, while the other keeps us humble."[iii] God's truth about us is that we are not failures, while our own opinion of ourselves is that we have trouble standing up straight and acknowledging our nobility and our responsibility. Both opinions have their truth, claims Julian, but God's is better. And from there our joy derives. From our self-doubt a certain humility obtains, however, and that has its place as well.

In a non-dualistic awareness, paradox and humor will always play an important part. Both are reminders that life is not one-dimensional; laughter has its place in a both/and world. Laughing at our condition and circumstances can itself express a kind of humility. "Both perspectives" can be true at the same time, she assures us.

Julian reminds us that the soul has two duties to perform. The one

---

[i] S 142.
[ii] S 160.
[iii] S 219.

is that "we must reverently wonder and be surprised." This names clearly the *via positiva*: reverence, wonder, awe and surprise. She continues: "the other is we must gently let go and let be, always taking pleasure in God."[i] Our letting go and letting be is what we learn in practicing silence and meditation; but it is also what we learn in undergoing suffering and grieving. Both of these tasks are tasks of the *via negativa*. Notice that she advises us to learn a *gentle letting go* and *letting be* while keeping in mind pleasure—both ours and God's. It can be a pleasurable experience to undergo what Meister Eckhart calls "subtraction," saying "the soul grows by subtraction and not addition." Julian, like the entire creation spirituality lineage, is not preaching asceticism but a gentle letting go and letting be. It is not meant to be a violent separation but a gentle easing—not a command of the will so much as a "sinking" (Mechtild's word) and letting go.

In this regard, Julian is very much in tune with the teaching of Meister Eckhart who says:

> Asceticism is of no great importance. There is a better way to treat one's passions that to pile on oneself ascetic practices which so often reveal a great ego and create more, instead of less, self-consciousness. If you wish to discipline the flesh and make it a thousand times more subject, then *place on it the bridle of love*. Whoever has accepted this sweet burden of the bridle of love will attain more and come much further than all the penitential practices and mortifications that all the people in the world acting together could ever carry out. Whoever has found this way needs no other.[9]

A bridle, of course, is a steering instrument that one puts on a horse to guide it, so that the horse does not run wild. Eckhart, who came from a family of knights and horse people, insists that even the bridle must be a "bridle of love." In other words, no dualism! Love unites us to our passions, just as love unites the rider to his or her horse.

Julian reminds us that our mystical experiences of undergoing oneing and breakthrough, union and ecstasy, do not continue unabated when she

---

[i] D 78.

tells us that "seeing God in this life cannot be a continuous experience."[i] As the saying goes, "after ecstasy comes the laundry." This is one reason work balances and grounds our times of breakthroughs. We would go crazy if we were on a high twenty-four hours a day. We must find a rhythm between wonder, silence, suffering, letting go, letting be, committing, and working. Julian credits the Holy Spirit with helping us to find that rhythm, for the Holy Spirit, who is "the endless life living within us, makes us peaceful and at ease, harmonious and flexible."[ii] The goal is to find peace both in the light and the dark, good times and bad, joy and sorrow. The Holy Spirit co-creates such harmony with us, and it is our task to remain flexible.

Sometimes we go back and forth between the *via positiva* and *via negativa* such that "the mingling of both well-being and distress in us is so astonishing that we can hardly tell which state we or our neighbor are in. That's how astonishing it is!"[iii] But she, like Mechtild before her speaking of the red and white wine we drink in life, reminds us that "we stand in this mingling all our life" and that together, the *via negativa* and *via positiva* experiences create a whole. "The fact is that it is part of being whole both to feel God when God wants us to and to coexist with God with all our heart, soul and capability" when we face struggle.[iv] She calls us to take on the darkness "with all our heart, soul and capacity" and not to fall into idleness or lack of energy and purpose. To put up a good and an imaginative fight, allowing purification to happen in order to return to one's purpose. To learn to dance and live with the dialectic of joy and sorrow, but to persevere.

Julian names her own experience in wrestling with the mingling: "I saw God and sought God. I had God and failed to have God." The lesson learned? "This is, and should be, what life is all about, as I see it."[v] Life itself is a dance and a dialectic. Get used to it, she says!

Another way she describes the *via positiva* and *via negativa* is by saying that a part of our soul "is one with God, dwelling in the fullness of joy and peace." Another part, however, "takes form and suffers for the liberation

---

[i] D 78.
[ii] D 78.
[iii] D 87.
[iv] D 87.
[v] D 34.

of all beings."[i] Suffering is meant to be redemptive—that is, it can serve others. There is meaning in our suffering if we pay attention.

Saint Paul advises that we "pray constantly." Julian puts her own spin on that reality when she says, "God wants us to allow ourselves to see God constantly." Of course, that is not always possible but, nevertheless, "God wants to be seen and wants to be sought. God wants to be awaited and wants to be trusted."[ii] Trust is indeed vital for Julian.

---

[i] S 153.
[ii] D 35.

6

Trusting Our Sensuality

God is in our sensuality.—Julian

In addressing how to navigate a pandemic—or, indeed, the tribulations of life in general—Julian is realistic. She reminds us that "God did not say, 'you will not be tempted; you will not be troubled; you will not be distressed.'" Trouble, temptation, distress—the *via negativa*—is part of our life journeys whoever we are and wherever we find ourselves, whether amid a pandemic or a post-pandemic recovery. Julian continues: "What God said was, 'You shall not be overcome.'" (This was six centuries before the civil rights marching anthem.)

The Importance of Trust

Julian goes on: "God wants us to pay attention to these words and be strong in absolute trust, in both well and woe." Absolute trust—what is that? How strong and complete is that? She refuses us the option of mild trust or "maybe" trust, but rather insists on an *absolute* trust. Whether we experience the joys of the *via positiva* or the afflictions of the *via negativa*, trust is the underlying attitude. Trust is a key virtue for Julian. She adds, "Just as God loves and delights in us, it is his will that we love and delight in him, and fully trust in him, and all will be well."[i] From trust comes hope, and "all will be well," she promises.

---

[i] S 187.

To me trust carries two substantive meanings. The first is that trust is the primary meaning of the word *faith*, as used, for example, by Jesus in the gospels. "Go your way, your *trust* has saved you," he says often in scenarios where he heals people. Very often we have translated that word (*pisteuein* in Greek) as "faith," but the deeper meaning is "trust." Faith has come to mean other things, of course, such as a list of doctrines or dogmas to believe in—what Augustine called "intellectual assent." This was especially the case as Christianity became more heady and more responsible for law and order in a Christian empire and more eager to identify those orthodox "insiders" and heretic "outsiders." There is no substitute for trust, and clearly faith-as-dogmas is no substitute.

Trust names the basic psychology to the creation spirituality tradition, whereas fear names the more prominent psychology in the fall/redemption tradition. For example, as psychologist William Eckhardt has demonstrated in his substantive study on the psychology of compassion, compassion is a function of faith [read *trust*] in human nature, while compulsion is a function of lack of faith in human nature."[1] With Julian, so thoroughly a creation spirituality theologian and so committed to compassion, trust is also a primary attribute to her psychology. But trust is not only extended to our attitudes toward human nature, but to the universe as a whole. Albert Einstein once asked the question: "What is the most important question to ask in life?" And he answered: "Is the universe a friendly place or not?" In other words, can we trust the universe? Well, after 13.8 billion years, we can surmise that it has been quite friendly to the earth and all her creatures, humans included.

Trust also lies at the center of Israel's wisdom tradition, which scholars today agree is the tradition of the historical Jesus. This creation-centered school of thought begins with the cosmos and the goodness of nature—not with human sin or human books, however holy they may be. Wisdom scholars remind us how central trust is to that tradition. Lutheran biblical scholar Gerhard von Rad writes that the world the Creator has made "is a world that is thoroughly worthy of trust."[2] And Catholic biblical scholar Roland Murphy says that the scriptures make clear that the two most important factors in learning wisdom are "an openness to experience and nature and a basic trust." Indeed, "the reason for this openness is trust."[3]

It is for good reason, then, that Julian speaks often and insightfully about trust.

In his essay on "The Trusted Creature," the contemporary biblical scholar Walter Brueggemann traces the growth of King David's life of faith as a growth *in trust*. David turned his back on some of the pieties of his ancestors and gave birth to "a radical innovation which will not be subsumed under the already existing structures" of his kingdom. He brings, therefore, "a new perspective toward human history, human responsibility, human caring, human deciding" that will "overturn conventional notions of what is sacred."[4] Jesus did a similar thing in his day by his teachings.

But even more than David's trust was his awareness of being *entrusted* with responsibility for history. "What God does first and best and most is to trust his people with their moment in history. He trusts his people to do what must be done for the sake of his whole community." Such trust lies at the heart of the wisdom literature.

Yahweh called and "trusted David and turned him loose to make what he can of the great trust vested in him, without reservation. . . . The picture which emerges is a man who knew himself a fully free man, fully responsible, fully involved but fully his own. . . . David thus embodies the best of wisdom theology."[5]

Courage, Faith, and Trust

Civil rights leader Reverend Fred Shuttlesworth was a man who felt himself entrusted with his moment in history. He was very much a fully free and fully responsible leader, and from him I learned a very deep lesson about trust and bravery. Fred was a street minister in Birmingham, Alabama, during the fierce battles fought during the Civil Rights movement. Being the visible leader he was, he was beaten three times with chains by the Ku Klux Klan, his two young children were arrested by Sheriff Connor and put in jail, and his house was blown up with him in it. The roof caved in, but he walked out unharmed.

I was invited to share a public dialogue with him on ecology and racism in the Birmingham Civil Rights Institute, a new museum located across the street from the Baptist church where four young girls were blown up by the KKK during Sunday morning church services. Just before our dialogue began, he and I shared a sandwich in a back room, and I said to him, "Fred, I have one question for you. Where did you get your courage?" I will never forget his answer: "You may call it courage," he said, "but I call it trust. When they blew up my house, and the whole roof caved in, and I walked out okay, I said to myself, 'They can't kill me. Oh, some day they may kill my body, but they can't kill my soul, and they can't kill the movement.'"

Needless to say, I learned something that day, something real and deep about courage and trust. Courage *comes from* trust. It builds on it. This lesson did not come from a book or a dictionary; it came from a practitioner, a saint, who walked his talk even in the midst of danger. Notice, too, that he was less worried about his own life than about the movement to which he had committed himself. Community came first for him.

Thomas Aquinas recognized an important link between trust, courage, and magnanimity, our capacity to grow big souls and do great things. This is how he puts it: "Courage, properly speaking, strengthens a person to take on good tasks. This is why trust pertains more properly to magnanimity than to courage."[6] Note that Fred Shuttlesworth's witness was to courage but also to magnanimity, because he took on good and great tasks in the face of injustice and racism. Let us not underestimate trust, Julian says. As does Fred Shuttlesworth.

Julian develops her teaching on our learning to trust life and God when she says: "We should desire to regard our Lord with wondering reverence rather than fear, loving God gently and trusting with all we are capable of." Notice that trust and love are the opposite of fear, and she subtly distinguishes between "fear of God" and "wondering reverence," which is a kind of "chaste fear" or awe. Trust and gentleness go together.

Furthermore, "when we regard God with awe and love God gently, our trust is never in vain. The more we trust, and the more powerful this trust, the more we please and praise our Lord whom we trust in."[i] You can trust trust, Julian tells us, and it will grow. It is like a muscle that requires exercise to develop.

So essential is trust to Julian that she refers to the theme often. For example, she recognizes that the true meaning of faith is trust when she

---

[i] D 122.

says: "Faith is nothing else but a right understanding of our being—trusting and allowing things to be. A right understanding that we are in God and God whom we do not see is in us."[i] For Julian, a bottom line of faith (and trust) is *panentheism*. The nearness of God who is in us and in whom we also dwell.

She encourages a generous trust when she says, "It is the will of the Lord that our prayer and our trust be large."[ii] Are there limits to trust when you are dealing with the Creator and the Spirit Maker of the universe itself? We often apply limits, she observes, and we often fall short in trust. She confesses to that shortcoming herself. "Often our trust is not full. We are not certain that God hears us because we consider ourselves worthless and as nothing. This is ridiculous and the cause of our weakness. I have felt this way myself."[iii] So doubts about trust arise often. Psychology tells us that trust is best learned as children at a very early age, and where there is abuse or trauma, trust is often ruptured. Julian attributes lack of trust to lack of self-worth. Good parenting and a healthy culture breed trust. Bad parenting and an unhealthy environment kill it—or at least suspend it. Love teaches trust. As Julian puts it, "we are all one in God's sight. We must trust and be glad for everything."[iv] So trust is related to gratitude as well.

Julian assures us that "when we trust that God is working within us, . . . he opens the eyes of our understanding and gives us insight."[v] Again, she relates trust to our believing in the nearness of divinity, who is within us as well as all around us. Panentheism for Julian is a practice, not just a handy theological concept. It is something we learn to live with, something to be present to in silence as well as in action. Life is bright, and it is dark, and we saw Julian name this dance and dialectic in the previous chapter. She writes: "Our Beloved wants us to trust that he is always with us. . . . He dwells eternally with us inside our own souls, directing and protecting

---

[i] D 89.

[ii] D 71.

[iii] D 67.

[iv] D 52.

[v] S 142.

us."[i] Even when life is a "muddle," we are protected and can trust in the divine so close to us.

In emphasizing trust, Julian finds herself in very good company. Trust constitutes the psychology of wisdom literature, of the royal persons as personified by David, of the Yahwist author of the Hebrew Bible, of Jesus, of Hildegard of Bingen who said "trust shows the way," and of Meister Eckhart who said that "you can never trust God too much" and then asks the question: "Why is it that some people do not bear fruit?" What holds people back from their own creativity? His answer: "It is because they have no trust either in God or in themselves."[7] We are meant to trust ourselves in order to make the contributions that we are here to make. Trust, not fear, marks the divine feminine. Julian calls on trusting "Christ, who is our true mother, completely,"[ii] and she thereby reminds us that trust is often learned from our mothers.

Trusting our Bodies

Integral to learning trust—including trust of nature and of the cosmos—is learning trust about *our bodies*, which are, after all, the product of nature and our link to the cosmos itself. Sixty percent of the trillions upon trillions of atoms in our bodies were birthed in the original fireball 13.8 billion years ago—that is, our bodies are *cosmic bodies*. The remaining elements of our bodies were birthed in a supernova explosion about five billion years ago. Our bodies link us to our past, to our human ancestors through our DNA, but also to our fireball and galactic and supernova ancestors, including hydrogen, helium, carbon, magnesium, oxygen, sulfur, and much more.

Yet instead of celebrating our bodies and the wondrous history they carry in them, we are often taught that the body is something to be afraid of or something to judge according to norms of "beauty" more often than not manufactured by advertising moguls with a narrow and bogus version of beauty in mind. Body hatred and body shaming abound, and body diseases such as bulimia and anorexia abound with them. How much opioid addiction begins with physical pain in our bodies that we can't

---

[i] S 143.
[ii] S 159.

imagine ourselves handling? How much self-hatred, sadness, and despair lie behind the drug addictions devastating middle America? Many are the young today who indulge in cutting themselves or attempting suicide.

How much industrial agriculture is bad for our bodies and those of our children? Instead of honoring our bodies and caring for them properly by exercising smartly and eating wisely, we are set up for violence toward our bodies by powerful economic forces that flood us with nonstop advertisements that seduce us into consuming foods loaded with sugars and chemicals that our bodies cannot process. Obesity and diabetes, too, are not just a crisis in America, one that we export around the world, but they provide a business model on which food corporations are making billions.

Julian of Norwich would have none of this denigration of the body. She insisted on non-dualism between matter and spirit, soul, substance, and spirituality. Her non-dualistic consciousness expresses itself forcefully on this issue. She insists: "God is in our sensuality [and] I understood that our sensuality is grounded in Nature, in Compassion and in Grace."[i] It is through our bodies and our sensual knowledge that we learn about goodness and grace. "This enables us to receive gifts that lead to everlasting life. For I saw that in our sensuality God is."[ii] There exists a "beautiful oneing that was made by God between the body and the soul."[iii] The "oneing" that Julian celebrated so richly, as we saw in chapters 3 and 5 above, is now applied to the oneing of body and soul, the spiritual and the sensual.

For Julian, the divine presence, what Eckhart called the "spark of the soul" is a special place in us where the divine dwells and acts. "In the same point that our soul is made sensual, in the same spot is the City of God established from without beginning. God comes into this seat and never will remove it."[iv]

For Julian, God is a kind of "glue" knitting our soul and body together, spirit and matter in one. She writes: "God is the ground in which our soul stands and God is the means whereby our Substance and our Sensuality

---

[i] S 1552.

[ii] D 92.

[iii] D 93.

[iv] D 94.

are kept together so as to never be apart."[i] She stands up against all dualisms, so many of which traveled in past centuries between one Platonic theologian to another (Augustine, for instance, pronouncing that "spirit is whatever is not matter" or Plato insisting that matter is an illusion). In Julian's worldview, as in Aquinas's, spirit is the "élan in everything" and that includes matter in all its variations and manifestations. Julian's non-dualism and respect for matter and sensuality places her squarely in the lineage of feminists (including Thomas Aquinas, whom I call a "proto-feminist") who have been battling dualism for centuries.

Years ago, after my book *Whee! We, wee All the Way Home: Toward a Sensual, Prophetic Spirituality* appeared, I received a phone call from a former professor, a Dominican priest and medievalist with whom I had studied during my three years of training in philosophy. He was quite renowned and had been "elevated" to be a professor at Toronto's prestigious Pontifical Institute of Mediaeval Studies. I remember his call vividly, even though it was some thirty-nine years ago, for he was a strict teacher who had taught me in many classes, oversaw my bachelor's thesis, and pumped me full of the details about scholarly rules, footnotes, and the rest (he was German, after all!). The call went something like this: "Matthew, you were always one of my best students, and I have followed your work the past few years but having seen your new book—where you put the words 'sensual' and 'spiritual' in the same sentence, I want to tell you this: I will never speak to you again." He hung up the phone. And never spoke to me again.

Now the irony in this is at least twofold. First, his "specialty" was fourteenth-century science. But Julian was from the fourteenth century! Granted, science was not her domain, but it was clear that he had never even read Julian of Norwich, a champion of spirituality and sensuality. It dawned on me that likely very few (male) scholars have bothered to read the women mystics over the years. At the time, I happened to be teaching at Barat College, an all-women's college, and I was learning daily the price that women have been paying for centuries—having their bodies put down, judged, and otherwise abused. All this has happened under a patriarchal ideology of spirit vs. matter and sensuality vs. spirituality.

Secondly, this scholar was a Dominican and admirer supposedly of Thomas Aquinas, one who actually wrote a worthwhile book about

---

[i] D 95.

him—yet he seems not to have internalized anything of the *communio mirabilis* or "wonderful communion" of union of body and soul that Aquinas celebrates. "Sensuality is the name given the sensitive appetite," he writes, "[which is] one of the perfections of animal nature that is included in human nature. . . . I understand the sensitive appetite and passions to be the subject and seat of the virtues."[8]

I learned several lessons from this sad encounter with a former mentor of mine, but the most pertinent was that Julian, like Aquinas, was a pioneer who insisted on the non-dualism of spirit and matter, body and soul, substance and sensuality—and this means that she was (and is) a threat to many. She writes that God has forged a "glorious unity between the soul and the body."[i] For patriarchal mindsets, such talk is like throwing holy water on the devil—much hissing and smoke and gnashing of teeth ensues.

This story alone may help explain why it took three hundred years to get her book published, and why her work has been ignored for subsequent centuries. Here, too, she was taking on patriarchy with a vengeance.

Allow me to give one more example of a patriarchal relationship to the body, this from Cardinal Ratzinger, who eventually became Pope Benedict XVI. When he ran the Congregation for the Doctrine of the Faith (formerly the "Office of the Holy Inquisition"), Ratzinger published a document declaring that Christians should not learn yoga because it might get you too much in touch with your body! I suspect Julian would have a few words to say about that. How I pity those who cannot grasp sensuality and spirituality as one process.

Julian teaches that "until our soul is in its full powers we cannot at all be whole." What does it mean that our souls come into their full powers? She tells us. It means we overcome our dualisms—yes, patriarchy's dualisms. "By this I mean when our Sensuality is connected to our Substance we are made whole." And she recognizes this reunion of soul and body as part of the accomplishment of Christ's sufferings and our own. The journey into pain and suffering can rid us of our suspicion of body and matter and bring us back to wholeness.[ii]

She elaborates: "Both our Substance and Sensuality together may rightly be called our Soul. That is because they are both oned in God."

---

[i] S 152.
[ii] D 96.

79

Notice that, rather than arousing fear for our bodies or disgrace or shame, she insists how integral to our being one with God is our substance, sensuality, and soul being one with God. Non-dualism is everywhere—as much in our bodies as in our minds or consciousness. It is all one. Her teaching very much echoes that of Aquinas, who just a century earlier taught that the human person is more fully human *with one's body than outside it* and "the soul is more like God when united to the body than when separated from it."9

Furthermore, this was God's intention: "God willed that we have a twofold nature: sensual and spiritual."i In addition, says Julian, "our sensuality is the beautiful City in which our Lord Jesus sits and in which He is enclosed." We share Jesus's nature in this regard for "our substance— of the same nature as Jesus's—is also enclosed in him with the blessed soul of Christ sitting restfully in the Godhead." Here she reintroduces the concept of a Christological panentheism that we saw earlier. The very meaning of the incarnation is that "when God was knitted to our body in the Virgin's womb, God took our Sensuality and oned it to our Substance."ii She likes to talk of how our soul is "knitted" to our body and we are "knit to God in creation."iii Julian invokes the example of "knitting" so frequently that I suspect she had become quite adept at knitting in her cell.

Julian is not abstract about coming to grips with our human and sensual nature—she actually celebrates how our going to the bathroom is a task of co-creating with God: "Food is shut in within our bodies as in a very beautiful purse. When necessity calls, the purse opens and then shuts again, in the most fitting way. And it is God who does this." Yes, our undergoing our natural functions, which are indeed designed by God, is itself a God-function. We are co-creators indeed. She tells us why she is so sure of this, "because I was shown that the Goodness of God permeates us even in our humblest needs." Notice how she brings her entire theology and metaphysis of goodness to the natural processes of our life—it is a good thing to undergo a healthy bowel movement (or piss, for that matter) and Julian is neither prissy nor self-conscious about declaring both as a celebration of our health and of nature's (and therefore

---

i S 156.

ii D 99.

iii S 157.

God's) goodness. Indeed, as is obvious, if we are blocked up and cannot perform our natural functions, that is a sign of ill health. In speaking of our "humblest needs" in the context of what goes on in the privy, Julian returns to the root meaning of humility, which is earth (*humus* being the Latin word for "earth").

Consider, too, that going to the bathroom when living in a walled-in cell was less than commodious (no pun intended). Julian had to wait for someone to empty her commode. Odors likely hung around for a while, smells that were not always pleasant. In short, bodily needs were not easy or pleasing in her chosen lifestyle, but rather than complain, she makes a beautiful poem about the practice. She surely practices what she preaches about the goodness of nature.

Julian continues in her meditation on the holiness of our bathroom habits when she proclaims: "God does not despise creation, nor does God disdain to serve us in the simplest function that belongs to our bodies in nature." Do we at times despise creation? We do so when we ignore our bodies. Does our culture at times? Is denying climate change a form of despising creation? Here Julian applies principles that we considered previously in chapter 3 about God's love of nature and presence in it. This becomes the basis for her celebration of our sensuality and spirituality, of our everyday natural functions being sacred and spiritual functions as well.

Julian strives to bring body and soul, matter and spirit, into that "glorious unity between the soul and the body" that God has forged in us, echoing that "wonderful communion" phrase that Aquinas described.[i] She continues: "As the body is clothed in cloth and the muscles in the skin and the bones in the muscles and the heart in the chest, so are we body and soul, clothed in the Goodness of God and enclosed."[ii] The panentheistic imagery of enclosure that we have seen so often when Julian addresses our relationship with the divine is here reoriented to our relationship to our own bodies. Body, muscles, bones, heart, are all celebrated along with our clothes, skin, and chest. This is body awareness; this is creation spirituality. Yes, nature is grace, and grace is nature.

Julian is not alone in honoring the marriage of our sensuality and spiritualty, souls and bodies. Her elder sisters Hildegard and Mechtild also

---

[i] S 152.
[ii] D 29.

celebrated the godliness of earthiness. Says Hildegard: "Holy persons draw to themselves all that is earthly. . . . The earth is at the same time mother, she is mother of all that is natural, mother of all that is human. She is the mother of all, for contained in her are the seeds of all."[10] It is interesting that Hildegard, like Julian, moves from earthiness and humility directly to motherhood and a sense of the sacred earth as mother.

Awareness of body and honoring the holiness of it are integral to a healthy feminist view of the world. We also find such teachings in Mechtild of Magdeburg, who tells us:

> Do not disdain your body.
> For the soul is just a safe in its body
> as in the Kingdom of Heaven—
> though not so certain.
> It is just as daring—
> but not so strong.
> Just as powerful—
> but not so constant.
> Just as loving—
> but not so joyful,
> just as gentle—
> but not so rich,
> just as holy—
> but not yet so sinless,
> just as content—
> but not so complete.[11]

Our culture has passed on the message to many women and men alike that we ought to "disdain" our bodies. This disdain derives from a disparagement of our sensuality and earthiness, and it manifests itself also in our aggressive relationship to the earth, extracting so many resources while giving so little care in return. It is also present in our denial of the suffering that we have inflicted on Mother Earth and the subsequent climate change that we ignore at our peril. Extinction stands before us because we hate body and earth. Julian's teachings demand to be heard.

Mechtild, like Julian, celebrates the holiness of all earthy creatures when she proclaims: "I bless God in my heart without ceasing for every earthly thing."[12] Creatures do not take us from the divine nor exalt our egos—quite the opposite. "The manifold delight I learn to take in earthly things can never drive me from my love. For in the nobility of creatures, in their beauty and their usefulness, I will love God—and not myself!"[13] Such humility tames the ego. Respect for the rest of creation is a sign of wisdom in Mechtild's eyes, for "the truly wise person kneels at the feet of all creatures."[14]

Julian also finds support from her brother Francis of Assisi, who in his celebrated "Canticle of Creatures" also celebrated "Sister Earth, our Mother, who feeds us in her sovereignty and produces various fruits and colored flowers and herbs."[15] Her brother Meister Eckhart declares that "the soul loves the body," and in so doing is very much in tune with Julian's and Aquinas's insistence on the non-dualism between body and soul, spirit and matter.

Dualism has everything to do with the oppression of women. Julian addresses that fundamental reality in her resistance against it. Consider the observation and vision by Adrienne Rich in the afterword to her study of motherhood:

> I know no woman—virgin, mother, lesbian, married, celibate—whether she earns her keep as a housewife, a cocktail waitress or a scanner of brain waves—for whom her body is not a fundamental problem.
>
> The fear and hatred of our bodies has often crippled our brains. . . . We have tended either to *become* our bodies—blindly, slavishly, in obedience to male theories about us—or to try to exist in spite of them.
>
> The repossession by women of our bodies will bring far more essential change to humans society than the seizing of the means of production by workers. . . . We need to imagine a world in which every woman is the presiding genius of her own body. In such a world women will truly create new life, bringing forth not only children (if and as we choose) but the visions, and the thinking, necessary

to sustain, console, and alter human existence—a new relationship to the universe.[16]

I see Julian as launching such a discussion in her teachings on sensuality and spirituality in the fourteenth century. Indeed, Julian is a strong sister to Adrienne Rich.

There is a direct relationship between the way we treat our bodies and the way we treat the body of Mother Earth, as poet, prophet, and farmer Wendell Berry states: "You cannot devalue the body and value the soul—or value anything else. The isolation of the body sets it into direct conflict with everything else in Creation. Nothing could be more absurd than to despise the body and yet yearn for its resurrection."[17] Here, too, we have a deep affirmation of Julian's love of sensuality and substance together, as she puts it. Berry tells us he is "groping for connections" between "the spirit and the body, the body and earth. . . . There is an uncanny resemblance between our behavior toward each other and our behavior toward the earth. Between our relation to our own sexuality and our relation to the reproductivity of the earth, for instance."[18] Julian, too, was "groping for these connections"—and she found them and laid them out for us seven centuries ago.

The Importance of Self-knowledge and Healthy Self-love

For Julian, "we can never know God until we first know clearly our own soul."[i] This is a familiar refrain from the mystics—that we know ourselves. It is also a useful contribution of contemporary psychology by which we can come to understand and criticize our "soul"—that is, our response to events and relationships. How to improve them and get to know ourselves better. How to survey our own shadow rather than run from it or project it onto others. How to explore who we are and what our motivations are; how to explore the wounds that we inherit from family or society so that they do not dictate who we are. To learn who our true self is and what is holding it back from our seeking to grow, mature, and expand. To distinguish our true self from our false self. Meister Eckhart, echoing St. Paul, speaks to this when he says: "The outward person is the old person,

---

[i] D 98.

the earthly person, the person of this world, who grows old 'from day to day.' His end is death. . . . The inward person, on the other hand, is the new person, the heavenly person, in whom God shines."[19]

Julian speaks to the reality of our true and better selves in contrast to our false selves when she criticizes herself—but not too much—as she also counsels. "I think it's important to speak about my weakness, misery and blindness."[i] Self-criticism is not absent from her writings. She keeps any tendencies to an inflated ego in check. When she first attributed a vision to delirium, she thought better of it afterward and chastised herself, "wretch that I am," but when the vision returned, she told herself it was not a hallucination. She was instructed to "accept it, believe it, trust in it, hold it close and allow it to comfort you, and you will not be overcome." She learned to "Give this truth an unshakable place" in her heart. This story very much confirms her teaching about the radical foundation of *trusting*.[ii]

Julian learned to forgive herself often, and she instructs us to do the same. God "wants us to forgive ourselves and let go of this unreasonable despondency and these fearful doubts."[iii] She alerts us to how "we often fail to see God and then we fall into ourselves and feel there is something wrong with us—that we are perverse and responsible for the entrance of sin into the world and all subsequent sins. These feelings affect us mentally and physically." The Holy Spirit pulls us out of such beating up on ourselves—or it ought to, she reminds us.[iv]

Yet she insists on putting self-awareness and criticism within the larger context of our nobility and goodness: "Astonishing and stately is our soul—the place where our Lord lives. Therefore God wants us to respond . . . rejoicing more in God's complete love than sorrowing over our frequent failings."[v] She hears God saying: "Do not accuse yourself too much, allowing your tribulation and woe to seem all your fault: for it is not my will that you be heavy or sorrowful imprudently."[vi] There is a pseudo-humility, or false meekness, that prevents our forgiving ourselves,

---

[i] S 181.

[ii] S 190f.

[iii] S 199.

[iv] D 78.

[v] D 128.

[vi] D 125.

and we must be on guard for that. "God wants *us* to forgive *our* sin instead of falling into a false meekness that is really a foul blindness and weakness due to fear."[i]

Again, being self-critical, she confesses to us that she has sometimes put herself down and seen herself as worthless—but in doing so, she is being "ridiculous." She says that "often our trust is not full. We are not certain that God hears us because we consider ourselves worthless and as nothing. This is ridiculous and the cause of our weakness. I have felt this way myself."[ii] While recognizing the reality of our missing the mark or "sinning," she warns us not to dwell on our mistakes. God wants to change the subject and move us from "foolishly dwelling on sinfulness" and instead calls us to joy and to "enjoy me and your liberation." Furthermore, we can flatter ourselves that the mistakes we make are so all-important when in fact, goodness reigns, not our sins, and therefore "my own sin will not hinder the working of God's goodness."[iii] Besides, "it would be contrary to nature to put blame on God or show any lack of trust because of *my* sin. Since God does not blame me."[iv] God does not hold a grudge.

Julian parts ways with certain church teachings that keep people in a state of guilt when she writes: "I knew by the common teaching of Holy Church and by my own feeling that the blame for our sins clings to us continually while we are on this earth." Notice that she alerts us to her having internalized the guilt that religion has taught her. All the more surprising, then, is the revelation that follows: "How amazing it was then to see our Lord God showing us no more blame than if we were as clean and whole as the angels in heaven!"[v] She steps back from church teachings that arouse guilt again when she exclaims: "Holy Church taught me that sinners are sometimes worthy of blame and wrath. But I could not see these in God in my showings."[vi]

Julian does not traffic in cheap guilt or shoddy shame, which so often furnish the foundation for sick religion and sick politics. Nor does she

---

[i] D 120.

[ii] D 67.

[iii] D 62.

[iv] D 50.

[v] D 83.

[vi] D 76.

countenance others to do so; indeed, she insists on our keeping the larger view of the goodness of our existence in mind when she says that "in spite of all our feelings of sorrow or well-bring, God wants us to understand and know by faith that we are more truly in heaven than on earth." Her sense of a realized eschatology, the presence of divine grace, refuses to disappear amid mistakes and evil—and even amid plagues and pandemic.

7

THE POWER OF LOVE OVER EVIL: A CALL TO WELLNESS

We were made for Love. . . . It amuses me that the Lord of Love overcomes the spirit of evil. —Julian

Previously we have seen Julian talk of an "endless love" that embraces us and all creation. For Julian, we are surrounded in love; love is everywhere. That seems to be a logical conclusion of a theology of panentheism, wherein all beings are swimming in an ocean of divinity and breathe the divine as fish breathe water. Grace is like that.

On Love and Longing

When Julian talks about love—and she does so often in a book that, after all, is named *Revelations of Divine Love*—she frequently speaks of *longing*. As she sees it, such longing is not just of us for the divine, but *the divine for us*. "Love makes God long for us," she declares.[i] "Just as there is a property in God of compassion and understanding, so also is there a property of thirst and longing."[ii] Christ, too, exhibits a longing for "the spiritual thirst of Christ is a love-longing that lasts and always will until we are all together whole in him."[iii]

---

[i] D 55.
[ii] D 55.
[iii] D 54.

This longing in God and in Christ for us is mutual—the longing goes both ways—and it can prove painful. "In this manner of longing and waiting, God wants us to do the same." Learning to wait while longing can be painful. "This is our natural penance—and the highest, as I see it. For this penance will never leave us until we are fulfilled and possess God to the fullest."[i] Longing is a dimension to love that manifests itself as a part of the *via negativa*. But what do we *do* in this in-between time when longing is not fulfilled? "God wants us to set our hearts away from the pain we feel into the joy we trust will be ours." Even here, trust shows the way. Joy can be just around the corner. Hope matters.

Julian recognizes love as our *liberation*, or salvation, when she writes: "We will never be blissfully liberated until we are at peace, and love, for that is our liberation."[ii] Peace and love liberate us, make us whole, save us. And our work is to pass that love along so others are liberated.

For Julian, as we saw in chapter 2, the search for and memory of goodness is primal. From goodness there arises both love and hope, and all love is a response to goodness (or at least to what we *perceive* as goodness). This is its attraction. To speak of goodness is to speak of love, and vice versa. It is a way of seeing the world, for beyond love lies goodness. "A person who is joyful has greater hope," observes Aquinas, thus underscoring the role of the *via positiva* in keeping hope alive.[1] Goodness, as Julian insists, can be found everywhere in nature. And where it is missing in human nature, it is our task to make it right again, to bring it alive in ourselves and others.

Here, as in so many places, Julian sounds like Thomas Aquinas, who defines sin as "misdirected love." This understanding is very Jewish, in fact, for in Hebrew the word for sin is an archery term that means "missing the mark." Aquinas draws the logical conclusion that even sin is an effort at love, an effort at seeking the good—albeit an off-centered one.

Love between the human and God is sure, for "God says: 'I love you, and you love me, and our love will never be divided in two: for your benefit I allow sin to fall to you against your will. I am taking care of you. Believe me.'"[iii] Julian teaches that love is born of fidelity and wisdom and love is "a delight in God completely steeped in wonder." Awe and wonder, the *via*

---

[i] D 129.
[ii] S 122.
[iii] D 13

89

positiva, are the origin of wonder that encompasses love. Indeed, "we were made for Love," insists Julian.[i] The character we develop, and the virtues we practice, are "the love that is shared"; they are the expression and "the gift of love in action."[ii] Love is not just about feeling—it leads to action. Without the action, there is no gift-giving.

Julian tells us that, far from imagining God as a judge or peeping Tom or a punitive father, the truth is much different. "God wants to be thought of as our Lover." She interprets this to mean that we are "so bound in love as if everything that has been done has been done for me. That is to say, the Love of God makes such a unity in us that when we see this unity no one is able to separate oneself from another."[iii] Oneing is at the heart of love, and love is at the heart of all our oneing. Indeed, she summarizes her entire experience of *Showings* and *Revelations of Divine Love* this way: "Throughout the entire time of my showings, I observed two things. One was that the divine love is boundless and will continue forever"—and this infused in her "an unshakable security" and sense of protection. The second observation was that she could love and take delight in the "common teaching" of the church community.[iv] She did not doubt that all her observations sat squarely within the Christian tradition. She did not see her teachings as outside the mainstream in any way.

On Love Combatting "the Spirit of Evil"

Another dimension to love for Julian is that love and goodness wage combat with evil. For all her insistence on our living our lives swimming in goodness, and therefore in love, in no way does Julian shut her eyes to what she calls "wickedness and evil." Rather, she sees goodness itself as a force that stands up to evil, that forms the matrix for everything, evil included. "When we see that the power of love overcomes the spirit of evil, it fills our hearts with comfort and joy." And laughter—she *laughed* at what she calls the adversary's impotence. "It amuses me that the Lord of Love overcomes

---

[i] D 74
[ii] S 222
[iii] D 113
[iv] S 113f.

the spirit of evil. I realize that God sees evil for what it is, and scorns it, and always will. God showed me that the spirit of evil is damned."[i]

Is it true that when we see love triumph over evil—for example, when Gandhi expelled the British colonizers through nonviolent means, or when Martin Luther King Jr. defeated segregation by the same loving means, or when Nelson Mandela overturned apartheid in South Africa, or when John Lewis led a march over a bridge, got beat up, but also got voting rights laws passed—do these stories not also fill our hearts with comfort, joy, and even laughter?

Evil does not have the last word in life, as Julian sees it. "The power of Christ's blessed passion is greater than all darkness. The Adversary is wicked, but he's impotent."[ii]

Overcoming evil is part of the work of the divine mother. "Christ Jesus, who does good over evil, is our true Mother. . . . Wickedness has been allowed to arise in opposition to that goodness." Goodness "transformed it all into goodness."[iii] Thus we enlist and extend the power of the *via positiva* to do combat with evil. "It is in our nature to reject evil, human nature is purely good and beautiful in itself. Grace gives us the strength to turn away from wickedness. Grace annihilates sin and restores human nature to its original, blessed, beautiful source, that is, God." We are not born in evil, nor are we destined for evil, but rather goodness is our destiny. We are born for beauty. "Doing evil is incomparably more wretched and painful than hell, for evil is the exact opposite of the beauty of our true nature. Not only is evil impure, but also unnatural."[iv]

Evil is not an abstraction in our time. It unveils its face in a stark way when policemen sit on a handcuffed black man for over eight minutes as he begs for his life and tries unsuccessfully to breathe. It is present when racism embeds itself in a justice system that incarcerates people of color far more severely than white people for similar crimes, in an educational system that is inferior for poor children and is not designed to appeal to the cultural strengths of minority communities (strengths such as creativity and justice-seeking). It is present when three times the numbers of people

---

[i] S 35.

[ii] S 34.

[iii] S 163.

[iv] S 173.

of color die at the hands of the coronavirus; when people of color must struggle much harder to get loans for starting businesses and buying a home; when schemes abound to deny minorities their voting rights; when governments sit on nuclear weapons that can destroy the world as we know it and scientists sell their souls dreaming up ways to do so; when climate change is ignored or covered up; when millions of species go extinct; when the wealthy receive tax cuts while the poor struggle; when a coronavirus is ignored or dismissed and that dismissal results in hundreds of thousands of deaths; when the media fans the flames of hate and division and lies. When all this is in the air, our times are not short of evil.

Julian had a frightful visitation from the spirit of evil in her sleep: "He snarled at me with a vicious expression revealing huge, nasty, gleaming teeth. He did not have a regular body, but held me by the throat with his hairy paws. He was trying to kill me, but he couldn't." She "trusted herself to God," and an intense heat rose along with a foul stench. "Everything is on fire!" she shouted, but others did not smell the stench or feel the heat that she felt. Ultimately, she was relieved to learn that "it was just the spirit of evil who had come to tempt me alone."[i] But her respite did not last for long.

> Then the fiend came again, with all his heat and his stink, and kept me very occupied. The odor was vile and painful, and the physical heat was terribly oppressive. . . . This all seemed to be meant to move me to despair. . . . The spirits of evil occupied me this way all night long until dawn. Then suddenly they were all gone. . . . Nothing was left but their odor, which lingered for quite a while. I scorned that fiend, and so I was delivered from him by virtue of Christ's passion. It is through this that the spirit of evil is overcome just as Christ said it would be.[ii]

The lesson that Julian took from this encounter with evil was that "our good God showed me the hatred in the spirit of evil. When I say 'the spirit of evil,' what I mean is everything that is counter to peace and love." The

---

[i] S 182f.
[ii] S 188f.

spirit of evil has great "hatred for our souls, which burns inside him as a perpetual fire of envy. But all the sorrow he tries to impose on us turns back on himself."[i] Are the fires of envy alive and well in our day, too—that is, envy between nations and peoples, races and sexes, classes and religions?

Yet evil is subject to goodness, and goodness trumps evil, for "God's will that we live in longing and rejoicing is so powerful, it made me realize that anything opposed to this cannot possibly come from him, but rather from the spirit of evil."[ii] The *via positiva* carries a weight more powerful than evil.

Matricide, Misogyny, and the Reality of Evil

Julian's fierce commitment to the divine feminine and deep love for the divine mother seems to stand in broad opposition to the oppression of women that still plagues so many cultures and institutions in our day. She offers medicine for the perennial oppression and subjugation of women in societies around the world.

Julian also sheds light on the killing—indeed, the *matricide*—of Mother Earth that we see all around us. Of all humanity's capacities for evil, it is hard to imagine anything quite so destructive as the way the earth is being subjugated and tortured, raped and murdered, just in our own lifetimes. The destruction of her forests and rainforests, her soil and oceans, her rivers and lakes, her glaciers and animals, her birds and insects, her microorganisms that feed the food chain in the oceans—all this is evidence of the killing of Mother Earth as we know (and need) her.

It is not just Mother Earth that is under duress, however, but women, too. Let it not be forgotten that in the midst of the COVID-19 pandemic, an older, white, male congressman from Florida called a thirty-year-old Latina congresswoman from the Bronx a "f***ing bitch" on the steps of the Capitol. To top it all off, he then gave a speech using his wife and two daughters as "proof" that he respected women—puckering up to cry as he invoked "my God" and "my country." This is what we may expect from a sentimentalist who, as Carl Jung pointed out, invariably harbors violence inside. Violence and sentimentalism go together. Beware of sentimental

---

[i] S 207.
[ii] S 218f.

93

pseudo-pities, whether religious or political (both of which are so often wrapped up as "patriotic"). Judge people by their actions, not their tears.

Yet not a single member of his political party spoke up against the diatribe. Women across the country responded by saying they, too, had experienced such language and attacks. Indeed, my sister and my niece volunteered that information immediately on hearing of the incident. And my sister added, "I know no women who have NOT had that experience."

The "war on women" is not that different from the war on Mother Earth. The patriarchal heart, the reptilian brain, must dominate and subjugate—at least until it undergoes a conversion experience. The same political party that denies climate change also houses this misogynist congressman and his sentimental piety that hides behind the skirts of the women of his family when he is called out for his violence. His president and so many of his fellow party members share the same ways of being. Such hatred of the feminine cannot be denied, nor can it be allowed to continue and reign in the halls of power. It begs for the light of truth to be shined on it, revealing it for the falsehood that it is.

Julian is a truth-teller who shines a bright light on the need for feminine wisdom. Her insistence on balancing gender-talk about God is so profound and powerful for our time. Her entire theology celebrates non-dualism and rejects dualisms of all kinds. She honors the sacred marriages of nature and grace, creation and God, sensuality and spirituality, body and soul, earth and sky, masculine and feminine, that in turn offer the antidote to such attacks on women, the body, and Mother Earth. Julian does not carry within herself the deep taint of patriarchy and the evil that accompanies it; she has quite consciously moved beyond all that.

Neither does she carry within herself the immense burden of "fatalistic self-hatred" that Adrienne Rich observes in patriarchal cultures. Indeed, there is nothing fatalistic about Julian at all—not even in a time of dire destruction by the plague. She chooses, rather, to dwell on the *goodness* of life and how humans can carry on that goodness. And she certainly harbors no "self-hatred" as she strives to find herself, love herself, trust herself, and share herself and her truth by disclosing her wisdom in writing two books.

The "doctrine of discovery" whereby fifteenth- and sixteenth-century popes blessed the raiding of Africa for slaves and the colonizing and destruction of indigenous tribes around the world in the name of Christian empire is another treacherous example of matricide.[2] This pernicious doctrine effectively murders the "aboriginal mother love" that characterizes indigenous wisdom. If, as Jungian psychoanalyst and writer Clarissa Pinkola Estés insists, culture is indeed "the mother of mothers," then the murder and extermination of cultures is another act of matricide. Mother Earth and culture, the mother of mothers, are both at stake, even as reverence toward Pachamama is on the rise.

Let us apply Julian's teachings on motherhood to Mother Earth. As we saw in chapter 4, Hildegard was explicit in her language about Mother Earth, demanding that "the earth must not be destroyed." The destruction of the earth is the destruction of the feminine. Matricide is ecocide, and ecocide is matricide. Invasion of indigenous lands and destruction of their cultures, the spreading of viruses that killed millions of indigenous peoples—the outcomes were the same. History is filled with matricides of all kinds. Genocides, too.

Julian talked of besting the "fiend" that is the "spirit of evil." The fiend is the shadow in our histories, the shadow side of human cultures everywhere. Can we laugh at the shadow as Julian did? Can we move beyond it?

Kali as a Symbol for Our Times

Another way to speak of the presence of evil in our midst is to consider the shadow side of the Mother herself as depicted by the goddess Kali, the dark Mother of India. In their recent book, *Radical Regeneration: Birthing the New Human in the Age of Extinction,* Andrew Harvey, who was born and raised in India, and therapist Carolyn Baker instruct us on some deep teachings around Kali.

The ancient Hindu sages, we are told, "predicted the age in which we are now living. For them Kali Yuga represents the collapse of every kind of inner and outer coherence and personal and institutional forms of compassion, concern, and justice."[3] The current collapse of industrial civilization all around us seems to mirror this reality. We are rapidly moving toward a "lethal stage" when "Kali's dance will destroy ghastly amounts of human and animal life and a vast portion of the planet."

Yet they believe that the "global dark night crisis is not the end of humanity but the birth canal of the new human."[4] The dark night, including a "savage grace of annihilation" can lead us to a new stage in our evolutionary journey.

> The only way through the dark night, all evolutionary mystics agree, is through continuing trust in Divine love and total unconditional sustained surrender to the unknowable purposes of Divine intelligence. It is this trust and agonizing, increasingly humbling, surrender that finally unravels the false self with its hidden addiction to power and its blatant or subtle fantasies of "achievement," "status," and "prestige."[5]

They cite poet-farmer Wendell Berry, who says, "It may be that when we no longer know what to do, we have come to our real work, and when we no longer know which way to go, we have begun our real journey."[6]

John of the Cross wrote in one of his poems: "Love, it's all I do." Near the end of her book, Julian is shown the fuller meaning of her work in the following exchange:

It was said to me: "Do you wish to see clearly your Lord's meaning in these Showings? See it well.

> Love was your Lord's meaning.
> Who showed it to you? Love.
> What did you see? Love.
> Why was it shown? For Love."[i]

As we saw in chapter 5, "endless love" is afoot; it is ours to imbibe.

All Will Be Well

Thomas Aquinas links hope to trust because trust "furnishes a certain vigor to hope. For this reason, it is the opposite of fear, as is hope."[7] Trust and magnanimity revitalize us with energy and enthusiasm for good and

---

[i] D 134.

great tasks that in turn bring about hope. Eco-philosopher David Orr defines hope as "a verb with the sleeves rolled up." Julian would agree—hope comes when we undergo inner work, including the heavy lifting that comes when we undergo the dark night, as well as deep entry into goodness, joy, and awe. And it comes when we create good work that returns goodness to the world. This good work includes both our inner work and our work out in the world. Consider the life work of John Lewis, who is being remembered as I write this on the day of his burial. His memory and his courage give the rest of us hope.

Perhaps Julian's most remembered refrain is that "all will be well, all manner of things will be well." As we saw in considering her treatment of darkness and evil in chapter 1, as well as her encounter with evil in this chapter, Julian dismisses all wishful thinking and instead demands that we face the dark directly for what it is. At the same time, because she does not live exclusively in the world of human affairs, she is open to what lies deeper in us and what might come *after* the darkness of a pandemic. Might the annihilation we are passing through purify our minds, so polluted by the egomania of our culture including the nostalgia and compulsion to "return to normal" (whatever 'normal' was)? Who knows the possibilities that await a renewed humanity, one that has gone through the fire of the dark night together?

Is it possible to let go of our bloated defense budgets and patriarchal games long enough to invest in a different future, one that is more sane and sustainable? Is it imaginable to call a ceasefire in our war on Mother Earth to move from ecocide to embracing her and altering our harmful living habits? May we think about the children of the future, and not the egos of today? And may we do it in the nine years we have left, according to a 2019 United Nations report? Such a future would be inclusive of feminine wisdom and less beholden to patriarchy and its obsession with power games and the "fatalistic self-hatred" that comes with them. Might such a conversion experience be a good result born of a time of the coronavirus?

If so, then Julian's vision for the future holds promise. So committed is she to this mantra of hope that she repeats it on many occasions with slight variations. God speaks to her: "It is necessary that sin should exist, but all will be well, and all will be well, and every manner of thing will be well."[i] Sin, whether understood as merely missing the mark or outright evil, happens in history and in our own imperfect choices. But the bottom line is not about the bad news, but rather the good news that wellness *will* triumph, goodness *will* arise, and truth *will* redeem the falsehoods to which humans are prone. Is this wishful thinking?

On another occasion she informs us that "Our good Lord answered all my questions and doubts by saying with full energy: 'I can make all things well, I know how to make all things well, I desire to make all things well, I will make all things well, and you will see with your own eyes that every kind of thing will be well.'" She concludes that we should find peace in this teaching, since "God wants us to be enclosed in these words restfully and peacefully."[ii]

Julian names the two greatest "sicknesses" that humans hold within us that hold us back from our awakening and our survival. "God showed two sorts of sickness that we have: The one is our lack of ability to endure, or sloth—for we bear our toil and our pains heavily. The other is despair, or fearful awe. In general God showed sin in which *all sin* is comprehended, but in special I was shown only these two. They are the sins that cause the most pain and tempest us."[iii] Julian counsels us to face our acedia, our lack of energy to begin new things, and with it our despair and feelings of helplessness. She encourages us to roll up our sleeves and get to work— to both our inner work *and* our outer work, our spiritual work *and* our political work, our mystical *and* our prophetic work.

The second fault holding us back, according to Julian, is despair itself. It is the *via positiva* and a recovery of the sense of beauty and goodness that can awaken us from our inertia, acedia, and slumber and energize us anew. "Zeal," says Aquinas, "comes from an intense experience of the beauty of things." Yet the dark night and despair can be a gift if we follow its trajectory to a breakthrough moment.

In this context we can see in Julian's vision of the future not a naïve optimism or wishful thinking, or a spiritual bypass, but a deep call to action. She ensures us that "on the last day, we will clearly see in God the secret counsels that now are hidden from us. Then none of us will

---

[i] D 48.

[ii] D 53.

[iii] D 121.

be stirred to say: 'Lord, if we would have known these things, then all would have been well.' Instead we will all say with one voice: 'Lord, may you be blessed! For it is thus: It *is* well.'"[i] Our wellness as a species and the wellness of the earth itself, along with all its amazing species, is relative to our waking up and doing the work.

---

[i] D 135.

8

LIVING FULLY DURING AND BEYOND A PANDEMIC: SUMMARIZING JULIAN'S TEACHINGS

Charged with the quality of reverence and loving awe, we turn ourselves with all our might toward action —Julian

We have now journeyed through a sevenfold instruction from Julian, one that she edited and perfected from the age of thirty to near the end of her life some fifty-odd years later. Let us try here to boil down the essence of her teachings, following the structure of our seven chapters.

Chapter 1: Facing the Darkness

1. Don't flee the darkness; put truth before denial.
2. Take the occasion to examine one's goals and intentions, Why am I here? What and whom do I wish to serve?
3. Life is short. What to do with my life? How can I contribute especially when times are difficult?
4. Don't take life and time on earth for granted.
5. Don't be afraid to die. Go into many kinds of dying and letting go.
6. Do grief work.
7. Resist self-pity and victimhood. Prefer "getting better" and "enjoying life" to pining over feelings of pain.
8. Stay connected to your feelings, whether they be of joy or of sorrow.

9. Beware of numbing yourself with addictions, and be observant of their presence in society. Get a socially as well as personally critical grasp of who is profiting from such addictions.

10. Get used to a dance of both "mirth and mourning." Stay flexible.

11. Study what Julian and other mystics teach us about the dark night of the soul, the dark night of society (especially Mechtild and John of the Cross).

Chapter 2: Goodness, Joy, Awe

1. Fall in love with the world, in spite of history.

2. Remember how special and what a blessing it is to be here in an amazing universe on an amazing planet after an amazing journey of 13.8 billion years. See the bigger picture.

3. Drink in goodness. And remember: "The first good thing is the goodness of nature."

4. Do not become "too blind to comprehend the wondrous wisdom of God, too limited to grasp the power and goodness" of what is being revealed to us daily.

5. "God is the same thing as nature," and God is "the very essence of nature." Dwell on that.

6. "The goodness in nature is God."

7. God is "unending goodness" and an "endless goodness."

8. God undergoes "supreme delights" and "five supreme joys" in particular that he/she "wants us to rejoice in also."

9. We are all born into a "birthright of never-ending joy."

10. Healthy self-love is vital, and all we encounter in creation is "everything that God loves" also.

11. "To behold God in all things is to live in complete joy."

12. Our work (inner and outer) and our labor are holy. "Dig and ditch, toil and sweat" to "make sweet floods to run and noble and abundant fruit to spring" in your soul and soil. Let this "food and drink" of your labor become your "true worship."

13. Value awe. The first duty of the soul is "to reverently marvel." A "reverent awe is the proper response to the supreme beauty of the divine."

14. "This is the holiest prayer—the loving prayer of thanksgiving."

15. Thanksgiving leads to actions. "Charged with the quality of reverence and loving awe, we turn ourselves with all our might toward the actions" to which we are guided.

Chapter 3: The Oneing of God and Nature
1. The "first good thing [is] the goodness of nature."
2. "Light is the source of our life . . . light is God, our endless day."
3. "Nature and Grace are in harmony with each other. . . . Neither works without the other."
4. "God is the Ground, the Substance, the same thing as Naturehood."
5. "God is the true Father and Mother of Nature."
6. "Our ignorance of Love causes all the trouble."
7. "God never began to love us…we have been loved from without beginning."
8. Faith is trusting that "we are in God and God whom we do not see is in us."
9. "Between God and the soul there is no between."
10. Christ "embodies all humanity" and "represents the spiritual yearning in us all. Christ is all spiritual seekers and all spiritual seekers are Christ."
11. God says, "I am what makes you love. I am what makes you long and desire."
12. All nature is interdependent, and this is why "the sky and the earth failed at the time of Christ's dying because he too was part of nature."

Chapter 4: The Divine Feminine and the Motherhood of God
1. Mechtild of Magdeburg taught that "God is not only fatherly. God is also mother who lifts her loved child from the ground to her knee." We are "surrounded with the roundness of divine compassion"
2. Hildegard taught that we are "hugged and encircled by the mystery of God" who is "as round as a wheel."
3. A young woman spoke to Hildegard in a vision: Her name is Love. "It was from her that all of creation proceeded, since Love was the first. She made everything. She bought forth, in the beginning of all holiness, all creatures without any admixture of evil."

4. "God feels great delight to be our Father and God feels great delight to be our Mother."

5. Compassion "belongs to the motherhood in tender grace." Compassion "protects, increases our sensitivity, gives life and heals."

6. "The working of compassion keeps us in love." Justice is integral to compassion.

7. "God is Justice."

8. "A mother's service is nearest, readiest and surest."

9. "Jesus is our true Mother in whom we are endlessly carried and out of whom we will never come."

10. Christ is "our Mother of Mercy" who "restores and redeems us."

11. The divine feminine and motherhood of God are integral to the entire Trinity and Godhead.

12. Christ is divine Wisdom and that too bespeaks the divine feminine.

13. The Mother God suffers when Mother Earth suffers.

14. Stand up to patriarchal vengeance and wrath, for they are found in us but never in divinity.

Chapter 5: Tasting Non-dualism

1. "In our creation we were knit and oned to God." It is a "precious oneing."

2. We were created "luminous and noble" and we were "known and loved from without beginning."

3. Prayer "ones the soul to God," and so does contemplation.

4. We share the pain of Christ due to "a great oneing between Christ and us because when he was in pain, we were in pain."

5. There exists a "true oneing between the divine and the human."

6. Nothing separates us from Christ.

7. "We experience a wondrous mixture of well and woe," of "the glory of the Risen Christ and the misery of the Fallen Adam." The basic remedy during a pandemic is to live with this dialectic.

8. There is "cause for mirth and cause for mourning;" we are "elevated" and we "come tumbling down."

9. Expect to be confused—respond with "holy assent."

10. "Do not give in to our negative impulses. . . . We remain in this muddle all the days of our lives. But our Beloved wants us to trust that he is always with us."

11. Resist dualisms. We "partner with God" when we "weave and join" the *via positiva* and *via negativa* in life. It is a *via creativa* dance that we co-create with Divinity.

12. Our first duty in life is to "reverently wonder and be surprised." Thus, the *via positiva*.

13. Our second duty in life is to "gently let go and let be, always taking pleasure in God." Thus, the *via negativa*.

14. "Seeing God in this life cannot be a continuous experience." Find a rhythm therefore, and work with the Holy Spirit who "makes us peaceful and at ease, harmonious and flexible."

15. "The mingling of both well-being and distress in us is so astonishing that we can hardly tell which state we or our neighbor are in. That's how astonishing it is!"

Chapter 6: Trusting Our Sensuality

1. In a pandemic, "God does not say, 'you will not be tempted; you will not be troubled; you will not be distressed.' What God said was, 'You shall not be overcome.'"

2. "Listen to these words and be strong in absolute trust, in both well and woe." Consider Martin Luther King Jr., Fred Shuttlesworth, Dorothy Stang, and John Lewis for their trust giving birth to courage.

3. Trust is the basis of compassion and trust is the real meaning of *faith*.

4. Trust lies at the heart of wisdom literature, and the wisdom tradition is that of the historical Jesus.

5. Julian links trust and faith to panentheism: "Faith is nothing else but a right understanding of our being—trusting and allowing things to be. A right understanding that we are in God and God whom we do not see is in us."

6. Let your "trust be large." And "trust and be glad for everything."

7. Trust your body. "God is in our sensuality."

8. A "beautiful oneing was made by God between the body and the soul."

9. "God is the means whereby our Substance and our Sensuality are kept together so as to never be apart."

10. "God has forged a glorious union between the soul and the body."
11. Be at home with your body, for "God willed that we have a twofold nature: sensual and spiritual."
12. "The goodness of God permeates us even in our humblest needs," including going to the bathroom, which is in fact the work of God who "serves us even in our humblest needs." Here lies another example of the motherhood of God who serves us.
13. "God does not despise creation." Do we at times? Does our culture at times? Is denying climate change a form of despising creation?
14. Self-knowledge matters. Know yourself—especially your inner or true self—and resist those forces trying to make you into something you are not.
15. Be true to yourself. Also be self-critical—but not too much; don't overdo it.
16. Learn to forgive yourself and avoid a "false meekness that is really a foul blindness and weakness due to fear." Avoid fear.
17. To consider oneself "worthless and as nothing is ridiculous and the cause of our weakness. I have felt this way myself." Be strong.
18. Do not internalize oppressions that come your way. Resist those who want to dump blame, wrath, or shame upon you. Prefer agency to victimhood.

Chapter 7: The Power of Love Over Evil: A Call to Wellness

1. God and Christ thirst and long for us and want us to do the same toward them.
2. Liberation and salvation are the same things.
3. Goodness and love go together, love being a response to the good.
4. "We were made for Love."
5. "God wants to be thought of as our Lover."
6. Two lessons in Julian's writing these books: One is that "divine love is boundless and will continue forever."
7. The second is that Julian learned to "love and take delight" in the "common teaching" of the church community. In other words, she saw her theology as representing the mainstream of the Christian tradition.
8. Love overcomes evil.

9. "When we see that the power of love overcomes the spirit of evil, it fills our hearts with comfort and joy," as well as laughter.

10. Stand up against evil, for "it is in our nature to reject evil." Know and study the evil that is going on in one's day and address it.

11. Julian's person-to-person encounter with evil revealed to her "the hatred in the spirit of evil." She defines evil as "everything that is counter to peace and love."

12. Be strong and stand up to the evils of matricide and misogyny. Do so "with all one's heart, soul and capacity."

13. Stand up to the evil of patriarchy and its "fatalistic self-hatred" (Adrienne Rich).

14. Stand up to the evil found in the "doctrine of discovery" that justified slavery and indigenous genocides.

15. Critique the "fiend," or shadow side of history and cultures that perpetuate injustices.

16. "God is justice."

17. Trust adds vigor to hope and hope "is a verb with the sleeves rolled up." (David Orr) Therefore our hope is proportionate to our work, both inner and outer.

18. In that context Julian's promise that "all will be well" holds water. It is relative to our courage and trust to transform self and society from imbalance to balance, from dualisms to love, from matricide to motherlove, from excessive patriarchy, power-over and knowledge to wisdom, the divine feminine, a healthy masculinity that works for compassion and justice.

19. Two sicknesses hold us back: acedia and despair. "These two are the sins that cause the most pain and tempest us." The *via positiva* overcomes them, awe, goodness and joy, triumph over them.

Julian on the Four Paths: Another way to summarize her teachings

In this chapter we have summarized Julian's lessons from the previous seven chapters of this book. Another way to appreciate her teachings that are so intertwined with the creation spirituality tradition is to consider them in light of the Four Paths by which Creation Spirituality names the spiritual journey. We will do that here very succinctly.

Path One: The Via Positiva. The way of awe and wonder, joy and delight. Clearly this experience is richly developed in Chapter Two above and also in the chapters on the good in God and nature, panentheism, trust and oneing of God and nature in Chapters Three, Five and Six.

Path Two: The Via Negativa. Chapter One considers Julian's in-depth teaching on facing the shadow and undergoing the accompanying darkness but also resisting denial. In chapter Five we encounter Julian herself naming the Via Positiva and Via Negativa as the paths of "wellness and woe" that follow us all our lives.

Path Three: The Via Creativa. This is strongly treated in Chapter Four, the motherhood of God (Jung says creativity comes from "the realm of the mothers") as well as in Julian's books as a whole. *Showings* is a testimony to her art as meditation practice, her study, research and birthing of her book from the age of thirty onwards—and even of the English language through her writing.

Path Four: The Via Transformativa. In Chapter Four Julian treats compassion and justice and also in Chapter Seven she develops our need to become warriors and prophets who overcome the forces of evil with Love. Chapter Four is of course a deconstruction of one-sided patriarchal God imagery in order to usher in the divine feminine in all elements of divinity. The Conclusion and Epilogue chapters also speak to putting Julian's teachings into practice and employing her theology to stand up to oppression and injustice.

CONCLUSION

WHY JULIAN? WHY NOW?

John Lewis, the late and great prophet who lived in our midst for eighty fruitful years, left a farewell letter addressed to young people that was published as an op-ed in the *New York Times*. In that letter he passed on a brief reminder of his life, its struggles and defeats, its victories and challenges, and how as a teenager he was called by meeting Rosa Parks and Dr. Martin Luther King Jr. to a life of passion for justice. That life sent him to jail forty times and almost got him killed on several occasions, and then it called him to work in congress for thirty-three years, allowing him to make laws to support the work of justice. A life of justice is a life of compassion, as Julian knew. One lesson that Lewis left us in his farewell letter was this: "Study and learn the lessons of history. . . . Truth does not change."

I see this admonition to apply to this book on Julian of Norwich. She is an ancestor; to study her is to study history. But she is a formidable ancestor, a fountain of wisdom that was born in a cauldron of the greatest pandemic ever to hit Europe. The fact that she wrote (and then re-wrote twice) one book her entire lifetime is special, not only because it was the first book by a woman in English, but also because she nurtured it for so many years in contemplation and service. She was telling her truth, knowing, as Lewis knew in his parting letter, that she was gifting future generations.

The fact that her book was essentially ignored for centuries does not diminish its importance—quite the opposite. It makes us pause to ask: Why? Why was her book and life's work ignored for centuries? How would history, both religious and cultural history, have been changed if her book had been studied centuries ago? Would the Protestant Reformation have been necessary? Would the wiping out of indigenous cultures have been averted? Would slavery never have occurred? Would two world wars never have happened? Would schooling for children be funded properly? Would the destruction of the planet and climate change have been stopped in its tracks?

We learn about ourselves, our history and society by asking questions that expose the shadows in which we still live. To me it is obvious why her work was ignored, and in naming the obvious we name the shadows we have inherited from our ancestors.

First, she was ignored because she was a woman. Her contemporary, Geoffrey Chaucer, got his book published in 1476—the very first book off the very first printing press in England, in fact! But Julian was not just any woman. She was a deeply aware, conscious woman—and a self-affirming, confident woman who believed in her own experience as a woman. She wrote the first book in English by a woman, after all Why was it ignored? Let us meditate on that fact alone. And yet she kept writing it, reworking it. She did not just write about the importance of *trust*—she trusted. She trusted in her insights, intuitions, visions, experience, learning, and her right to tell the world about them. She trusted in her fifth chakra, her prophetic chakra.

The prophetic chakra is, of course, about speaking out, finding your voice, telling your truth and wisdom as you know it.

Julian found her voice—and wrote the first book in English by a woman. She speaks out about womanhood and about mothering and about the Divine Mother. She insists on the feminine side of God as imbuing not only God the Creator, but God the Liberator, and God the Spirit. She insists that the entire Trinity or whatever layers of divinity we dare to imagine are imbued with the divine feminine. Or ought to be.

She bakes into her entire book the constant theme of non-dualism and of "oneing." Sensuality and substance are one thing, which means our sexuality and spirituality are one thing, as well. She talks of the "glorious mingling" of body and soul, matter and spirit. She insists on the marriage of nature and God, on *panentheism* as the very meaning of faith, and on the marriage of God and the human (for we, too, are part of nature): "between God and the human there is no between."

Julian is an absolute champion of non-dualism. That means that she is a feminist, for as feminist theologian Rosemary Ruether has made clear, non-dualism is the essence of feminist thinking. This explains why she has been ignored, literally, for centuries. We were not ready for her. We were too engrossed with the masculine projects of empire building and "discovery" doctrines of raiding and destroying indigenous cultures of "mother love"; we were too busy chasing knowledge, at the expense of wisdom, for the power it brings to buttress our empires through science and technology, too preoccupied with creating capitalist behemoths that demanded we extract whatever goods we could from Mother Earth without asking any questions about paying Mother Earth—or future generations—back. We were too busy enslaving other peoples to keep that economic project going. We were too busy keeping women down and enslaved in more subtle forms of domination and disrespect. Matricide and misogyny ruled. Julian's feminism did not fit the patriarchal agenda at hand.

But today, thanks to the women's movement, the ecology movement, the Black Lives Matter movement, and to the facts of climate change and its child, the coronavirus, we are awakening to what we have done—and the price we have paid.

This is where Julian enters the picture. Her entire way of seeing the world is non-dualistic and feminist and she stands up to patriarchy (including the institutional church) in many instances. But subtly so—as a lover, not as a prosecutor.

The second principal reason Julian has been ignored for so many centuries, and why we were not ready for her, is that she is so thoroughly creation-centered in her theology that people did not understand her insistence that "God is in nature," that nature and grace are one, and that goodness is everywhere but "first of all in nature." When the agenda is to exploit nature for all the profits it can deliver, who wants to hear about the sacredness of nature? With the Black Death, as Thomas Berry has made clear, creation spirituality went out the window when it came to religion, and religion committed an ultimate act of anthropocentrism and narcissism when it essentially ripped out the first page of the Bible— which is all about cosmology—in favor of talking about the humans, their precious fall and salvation, original sin (which is nowhere in the Bible, by the way) and redemption. How ironic it is that one of the greatest champions of creation spirituality was effectively silenced at the very time when the pandemic that killed trust in nature raged.

But today we are ready to talk about the cosmos again, and to listen to science tell us about the cosmos, and to go deeper than the mere facts about the cosmos to its meaning. What does it mean that this earth, so abundant and beautiful and unique, so full of amazing creatures on land, sea, and air, was born 4.5 billion years ago in a cosmos of 13.8 billion years? And that our species has been invited on board after all these billions of years? Context is everything and our context is creation itself. Aquinas taught, that the most excellent thing in the universe is not the human but the universe itself and that "God wills that human beings exist for the sake of the perfection of the universe" and that "revelation comes in two volumes: Nature and the Bible."[1] He also encouraged meditation on nature since "by dwelling on creatures the mind is inflamed to love the divine goodness."[2] Julian studied nature, including human nature, in depth. How else could she say that "God is in nature" and that the goodness in things is God?

We have failed to get over our narcissism as a species and have become drugged and addicted to knowledge—at the expense of wisdom. We have elevated our power over and domination of Mother Earth, her other creatures, indigenous peoples and people of color whom we enslaved. Why? To serve the gods of our economy. In this process we became oblivious and forgetful of the radical wisdom of our creation centered ancestors. Julian is only one of them—but she stands out because she was so thoroughly conscious as a woman and because she kept the goodness and joy and delight in creation alive and central to her theology *even during a devastating pandemic.*

It has been my privilege to spend a lifetime pursuing this rich, but often abandoned, sometimes condemned, tradition called creation spirituality. Like John Lewis hearing Martin Luther King Jr. speak for the first time, I too found my vocation and life's work in following my mentor, the French Dominican and historian M.-D. Chenu, who called my attention to the two religious traditions in the West: the more dominant fall/redemption tradition and the creation-spirituality tradition. My life's work has been to explore the latter.

It has been a thrilling, sometimes challenging, journey. Two popes called my work "dangerous and deviant." History, however, has proven their papacies as the most corrupt since the Borgias. And a third, Pope Francis, has embraced creation spirituality in his fine encyclical on the environment, *Laudato Sí*, most of which was written by one of my students. I was silenced for a year and eventually thrown out of my order after thirty-four years for a book called *Original Blessing*, even though I have since uncovered the fact that Thomas Aquinas wrote about "original goodness" and "primal goodness," and Hildegard extolled "original wisdom."

In the process of mining my heritage for the creation spirituality tradition and drawing from the wisdom of other religious traditions that teach about the sacredness of creation, I have written three books on Hildegard of Bingen (who has since been named a saint and doctor of the church); three books on Meister Eckhart; and two books on Thomas Aquinas, also a saint and declared doctor of the church. (One provides a source book that translates for the first time all of his untranslated biblical commentaries and more).

And now I present this book on Julian. This is not my first foray into her work—I have shared her teachings with many over the years. But this book has allowed me a deeper journey into her soul and story, a journey for which I am grateful.

It is important to recognize that Julian did not drop out of the sky intellectually or spiritually. Julian, too, had her ancestors: Benedict, Hildegard, Francis, Aquinas, Mechtild, and Eckhart. Julian belongs in their league so grounded in the wisdom tradition of the Hebrew Bible that also nurtured the historical Jesus. I have no doubt whatsoever, after studying for this current book, that the biggest influences on Julian as an adult were Thomas Aquinas and Meister Eckhart, whether directly or indirectly. Remember that Aquinas, who was condemned by bishops in both Oxford and Paris less than a century before Julian was born, was condemned *for his non-dualism* (which, again, makes him a proto-feminist). But—and this cannot be emphasized enough—he was canonized a saint in 1323, less than twenty years before she was born. The excitement among the Dominicans in England must have been extreme.

Eckhart was condemned a week after he died about six years later, but the Dominicans smuggled his work into England and surely into Norwich along with works by John Tauler, his student and disciple. Julian must have been exposed to both.

All this adds up to this, however: that we are now ready, in the midst of a pandemic and climate change, to listen to Julian and her creation-centered mystics and prophets anew. Julian's time has arrived.

But that is not all. Patriarchy is dying in the light of the truths emerging about the subjugation of women around the world. Not only has matricide dominated long enough, as well as misogyny, but women and men are becoming daily more aware of the price we have paid. Julian is a champion of the divine feminine, and that includes the motherhood of God in all her manifestations. Here, too, Julian's voice has arrived at a perfect time.

Challenging the Theology Behind the Doctrine of Discovery

Let's be blunt. Though Augustine laid the groundwork for it in the fourth century with his misbegotten, unbiblical, and un-Jewish concept of original sin, the ascendency of the related doctrines of the fall and redemption in Western Christianity took flight with the bubonic plague. (The East rejected original sin outright.) This version of Christianity was a religion of fear, not trust; of anthropocentrism, not creation; of dominance, not love and compassion. Combined with the next century's second great plague, the ratcheting up of imperial ambitions buttressed by religious ideologies, fall/redemption religion took over. I am speaking, of course, of a metaphorical plague that we call "the age of discovery," which launched in the late fifteenth century and received support from several papal bulls collectively known as the "doctrine of discovery." These "doctrines" gave power to Christian kings and queens to confiscate lands and enslave peoples in Africa and the "New World" soon called the Americas. A fall/redemption theology was at the heart of this imperial conquest by "Christian" potentates. To be fair, these papal bulls were written in the context of Islamic ambitions in Africa, and they were intended, in part, to counterbalance them. That was the fuller political context for these bulls—to defend against Muslim efforts to convert African peoples.

Like a wildfire, with heat and high winds fanning the blaze, the doctrine of discovery spread over the next century with the Protestant reformers and the egotistical and "neurotic" (Stendahl) and introverted question "Am I saved?" that Protestantism preached and Roman Catholicism sold (along with indulgences which brought on the Protestant Reformation in many respects). This religion took western Christianity far off track—a detour away from love of creation and recognizing nature as a source of revelation and the divine, which Hildegard, Francis, Aquinas, Eckhart, and then Julian manage to steer directly through so well. Creation spirituality was effectively eradicated. Instead, a preoccupation with the fall and redemption served the agendas of colonialism and slavery, projecting falsehoods upon indigenous peoples who *were* living close to nature and understood the sacredness of nature. It nurtured collective evils of hysteria, genocide, and slavery.

Compare this teaching of fear of eternal damnation to the understanding from Aquinas, for example, that the essence of true religion is a "supreme gratitude." Compare it to Genesis 1—religion declares that creation and the cosmos are "good" and "very good" when humans join the goodness and original blessing that unfolds therein. Indeed, creation is sacred.

Of course, Aquinas is not alone—he stands on the shoulders of Benedict, Hildegard of Bingen, Francis, and others who saw the sacredness of creation as a starting point for religious practice. Humanity's imperfections and choices that "miss the mark"—the Jewish understanding of sin that Aquinas tweaks and defines as "misdirected love"—are to be remedied in the context of a sacred creation. Humans, too, are sacred, but, given such expansive minds and imaginations, we make choices that can readily take us beyond the best ends for our species and other species. We are that powerful. As Aquinas put it, one person can do more evil than all the other species put together. The other species are doing their best to propagate and survive and instruct their young. Few are involved in wiping out other species or poisoning the earth and climate in a manner that will render millions of species extinct for all time or in threatening all of earth with nuclear weapons.

It is in this growing gap between a creation-based spirituality and a human-based or fall/redemption-based spirituality that Julian appears. While all around her the plague was doing its destruction her entire life long, she does not break the covenant with the Jewish teachings of the goodness of nature including human nature. She is a champion of wisdom theology—indeed her entire theology is based on it, such as the statement that "wisdom is the mother of all good things" (Wisdom 7:11-12). Is this not clearly the very foundation of her metaphysics of goodness that so permeates her entire worldview? And source for her richly developed understanding of God as Mother? Julian turned such wisdom teachings over and over in her heart and mind her entire life long—and they make their way into every aspect of her "revelations of divine love."

Julian stands up bluntly and stoutly to any suggestions that denigrate nature in the name of religion. This was a very unpopular position to take in the time of a raging pandemic and a growing pessimism and an expanding patriarchy whose fires of reptilian brain dominance would be expanded by the greed and violence that accompanied the voyages to faraway lands in search of goods to buttress the ambitions of imperial powers. All this is very clear in the language and purpose of the papal bulls promulgating the doctrine of discovery, which were written between 1445 and 1494. Let us consider some of their language here.

In 1452 Pope Nicholas V issued the papal bull *Dum Diversas* to authorize Alfonso V of Portugal to redeem any "Saracens (Muslims) and pagans and any other non believers" to "perpetual slavery." Clearly, this facilitated the Portuguese slave trade from West Africa. In 1455, the same pope's bull *Romanus Pontifex* extended to Catholic nations of Europe dominion over discovered lands during the age of discovery. It encouraged the enslavement of native and non-Christian peoples in Africa and the New World. Calling the king to "invade, search out, capture, vanquish, and subdue all Saracens and pagans whatsoever, and other enemies of Christ wheresoever placed, and the kingdoms, dukedoms, principalities, dominions, possessions, and all moveable and immovable goods whatsoever held and possessed by them and to reduce their persons to perpetual slavery." Thus the global slave trade of the fifteenth and sixteenth centuries and the age of imperialism were buttressed with ecclesial backing—all of it in the name of a religion of redemption.[3]

In his bull *Inter Caetera*, issued in 1493, Pope Alexander VI embraced the Spanish kingdom's royal rulers, Queen Isabella and Ferdinand, and decreed that the "barbarous nations be overthrown and brought to the faith." Urging them to "spread the Christian rule," he heralded "our beloved son, Christopher Columbus" for "discovering very remote islands and even many land sites hitherto had not been discovered by others;

where dwell very many people living in peace, and, as reported, going unclothed, and not eating flesh." People who "believe in one God, the Creator in heaven." They were to be instructed "in the name of the Savior, our Lord Jesus Christ." Is it accurate to say a place and people have been "discovered" when they have lived there for thousands of years? And note that it is Christ as "savior" (not Christ as mother or teacher or justice or love) that justifies this charge. Notice, too, that the native peoples were *already living in peace.* Why did they need converting, then? And to what?

The pope invokes God as the God of empires that he declares to be God-given gifts, for God is the one "from whom empires and governments and all good things proceed" and the king and his minions should act for the sake of the "glory of all Christendom." He instructs the Christian empires not to step on one another's toes and should anyone disregard this bull "they will incur the wrath of Almighty God and of the blessed apostles Peter and Paul." Were Peter and Paul wrathful? And God too? Julian says she saw "no wrath in God," and that such divine wrath, therefore, is our own projection.[4]

In 1494, the Treaty of Tordesillas declared that only non-Christian lands could be colonized under the doctrine of discovery. In 1823, the doctrine of discovery became a concept of public international law expounded by the United States Supreme Court under the leadership of Chief Justice John Marshall "The doctrine has been primarily used to support decisions invalidating or ignoring aboriginal possession of land in favor of colonial or post-colonial governments."[5]

All this ambition and expansion and competition would hardly be a welcoming place for Julian's theology of the goodness of nature and of God; and of the motherhood of God that promotes compassion before all else; and true love and true justice and a God with no wrath. In short, a theology that prefers the mammal brain of kinship and motherhood and compassion to the reptilian brain of conquest and being Number One. Little wonder, then, that Julian's worldview was effectively shelved in favor of fall/redemption ideologies that, among other things, kept most individuals so tied up in knots for fear of damnation that they hardly questioned the dominant agendas of genocide, slavery, and wars. Patriarchy was on the loose. "Aboriginal mother love" as well as "God is delighted to be our mother" theologies were not welcome. No wonder, then, that

Julian's book was not published for hundreds of years—and that when it was published it was largely ignored! Women's energy was to go to the back of the bus in favor of imperial and patriarchal goals.

Julian taught and lived a creation-centered spirituality, and she clearly detected what was happening to religion insofar as it was embarking on a path of nature-hating and self-hating fatalism. She detected the flight from joy, awe, and goodness that was so established in wisdom theology. She recognized the excesses of patriarchy that was arising in Western religion. She stood against it and pointedly deconstructed it point by point: its pessimism, its dualism, its human-centeredness, its narcissism, and its oppression of women and nature. In many respects, she stood alone. Until today.

Julian rocks the world of religion—today and in her day. And with it, culture. Sociologist Robert Bellah points out that "no one has changed a great nation without appealing to its soul. . . . Culture is the key to revolution; religion is the key to culture."[6] Julian turns religion and Western culture inside-out and upside-down. With Hildegard, Francis, Aquinas, Mechtild, and Eckhart, she rewrites Christian spirituality and theology. Julian is a leader, and her companions just named are our guides. She stays true to the wisdom theology, which is a nature-based spirituality in Judaism that all scholars agree was the source of the historical Jesus's life and teachings. Julian, not papal bulls of discovery, speaks an authentic interpretation of the Jesus story and mission.

The doctrine of discovery promotes original sin in spades—original sin institutionalized, frozen, and projected onto all "non-believers." It served as the primary instrument in denouncing the primal religions of humankind. Without Christian redemption they were doomed—in this life *and the next!* Every Christian body today should formally renounce it, and the pope should burn it in St. Peter's Square for all the world to see. (It will be enough to burn only a copy of such bulls—the originals should be under glass in the esteemed Vatican library for all to see for centuries to come.)

Indeed, the creation spirituality of Hildegard and Aquinas, Francis, Eckhart, and Julian is the "theology of the future" as Fr. Bede Griffiths puts it. The God of goodness and awe, beauty and justice and love— isn't it time for that God again? The doctrine of discovery motivated the ships and soldiers to Africa and the Americas, serving the gods of empire, enslavement, and genocide, and even today continues to promote transnational profiteering and the despoiling of the earth and earth-based cultures. We are all suffering from the traumas of history this pernicious doctrine has unleashed. It is time to give the God/goddess of Wisdom and lover of nature her place. A place where wisdom, spirit, compassion, non-dualism, cosmos, panentheism, and Holy Mother Earth can all step forward. This adds up to a paradigm shift, where what used to be on the margins moves to the center. Julian is a source for this needed paradigm shift. Time is running out. That's why she has shown up.

Maybe we were not ready to hear from the creation mystics and prophets until now. Maybe we were not worthy. We had chosen a path of domination and destruction, of power-over instead of power-with, of wars and enslavement of African peoples and other reptilian games, of patriarchy and its distorted values, of rugged individualism and the survival of the fittest, rather than a path of interdependence and compassion, of gender balance and respect, of eco- and racial and economic justice. The very survival of our species, as well as millions of others and the rendering of our planet sustainable once again, calls for Julian's wisdom. Julian stands tall as a leader in the spiritual revolution of our time, and her wisdom has been ignored long enough. Her teachings, such as "the fullness of joy is our birthright," could indeed assist in the reinvention of our culture.

EPILOGUE

A PROPHET FOR THE TWENTY-FIRST CENTURY

We have considered Julian's non-dualism, her celebration of body and spirit together, or "sensuality and substance" in her words, her insistence on the goodness of nature and of sensuality, including, of course, our own. This is a direct attack on the crazy men who were, in her day, going village to village flagellating themselves. She does not shrink from letting us know what she thinks about that craziness. She also takes on the church approval of a vengeful and wrathful God—she sees no such thing, but rather sees *humans* as vengeful and wrathful. In other words, we are busy projecting onto divinity our own unexamined shadows and anger and bitterness. She explicitly rejects the punitive Father God of patriarchy and fundamentalism.

In our time of pandemic, we are working overtime and hoping for a vaccine. But perhaps we should also look deeper to the cause of the coronavirus—namely, climate change. *The cause lies deep in the rejection of nature as sacred,* in the exploitation of nature that capitalism and patriarchy have engaged in practically non-stop for centuries (slavery is part of that economic system). The denial of climate change and of science is part of this acting from the reptilian brain that patriarchy is famous for. So, too, the "fatalistic self-hatred" that Julian stands up to head-on. The matricide, the killing of Mother Earth and of indigenous religion, and misogyny are all part of that sick and toxic masculinity that we need some vaccine to protect us from.

Might I suggest this: maybe Julian of Norwich, and the rich tradition of creation spirituality that she carries in her bones, heart, and mind, from Jesus to Benedict, Hildegard, Francis, Aquinas, Mechtild, and Eckhart— maybe *she* is the vaccine that is truly needed today.

It is not enough to "return to normal" after this coronavirus, even if it does finally go away. That "normal" was far from healthy to begin with. It brought us climate change, the extinction of millions of species, with our own species on the cusp of extinction as well, and, of course, lots of denial in the name of those whose gods are Wall Street and multinational corporations. It brought us racism and sexism as a way of life, and it has distorted education and religion, politics, media, and economics. Who wants to return to that?

A pandemic is too important to waste. This pandemic is here to wake us up. To what? To a "new normal." One that honors the sacredness of the earth and of all its life forms. One that honors the divine feminine alongside a sacred masculine. One that honors the human body and its basic needs, along with those of the earth's body, and on that basis gives birth to a *new* body politic. One that does not put billionaires and the structures that create them on pedestals. And one that does not elect narcissistic politicians who incarnate the very meaning of fatalistic self-hatred by watching hundreds of thousands die with a shrug of the shoulder ("It is what it is").

Julian absolutely lays waste to a punitive Father God who operates on anger, punishment, and what she calls "vengeance." She found none of that in Divinity—only in humans (who project it onto Divinity)! A punitive Father God is the basis of all fundamentalism, whether found in the Taliban, Pat Robertson, or even the Vatican (as it was for thirty-four years under the über-patriarchal Popes John Paul II and Benedict XVI, who, as history will recall, brought back the Inquisition and condemned 108 theologians, driving most of them out of their livelihoods and sending fear into thinkers, many of whom rolled over and played dead, and essentially "killing theology" in the process, all the while holding up fascist religious leaders and the fascist orders they created). A punitive Father God feeds fascism the raw meat of vengeance and fear, hell and damnation, that invariably accompanies it.

The double blow that Julian delivers to patriarchy is to insist on the non-dualism of God and nature, God and humans, body and soul, sensuality and spirituality. Patriarchy thrives on dualism like a vampire thrives on blood. No wonder she was effectively ignored until the late twentieth century—her dismantling and deconstructing of patriarchy did not fit with the empire-building agendas of slavery, colonialism, genocide, and hatred of Mother Earth that we call *matricide* and has been driving western "civilization" since at least 1492.

Julian's love of nature is obviously connected to the goddess tradition— archaeologist Marija Gimbutas declared that "the Goddess in all her manifestations was a symbol of the unity of all life in Nature."[1] Julian's explicit redoing of the word "faith" to "trust" deconstructs the excessively heady intellectual thrust behind faith that defines faith as "assent" ("believe this or die"). The Christianity that invaded indigenous lands all over the world in the late fifteenth to seventeenth centuries could have used Julian's understanding of *faith as trust* (which, incidentally, was also Jesus's understanding of faith), rather than a twisted version of faith that conquistadores marched in while bearings flags of Christ and the cross. Trusting one's body, sensuality, and passions are at the basis of Julian's non-dualistic creation spirituality. It is trust—as psychologist William Eckhardt demonstrates in his book on a psychology of compassion—that builds compassion, not fear.

One modern-day martyr, Sister Dorothy Stang, gave her life for the forests of the Amazon and the peasants and indigenous peoples who lived there. She is a patron saint for the struggle to preserve the planet as we know it. She was also a student of creation spirituality, and therefore a descendant of Hildegard, Aquinas, Eckhart, and Julian.

Seven hundred years ago, we could not understand Julian and the creation spirituality lineage she carries with her. Today, with a women's movement, women active in scholarship and leadership, a Black Lives Matter movement, and an ecology and extinction rebellion movement— we can! And with matricide and misogyny staring us in the face, we must.

What, after all, is patriarchy if not the killing of the mother? Or the killing of compassion and the exaltation of the ego at all costs (those costs including war and revenge, projection, hatred, and the spending of $56,000 per second on death)? And roping in a punitive Father God to enlist divine sanction and approval?

Who is Julian if not the herald of the Return of the Mother principle of creativity and caring, compassion, justice, and strength? Maybe Julian is to the twenty-first century what Karl Marx (and Charles Dickens) were to the nineteenth. Just as Marx, tapping into his prophetic heritage, sounded a trumpet to expose the unethical shadow lurking in the façade of economic and industrial "progress," and just as Dickens shouted through characters suffering from the shadow side of capitalism, so, too, does Julian take on the privilege and dangers of patriarchy by deconstructing it. Instead of a punitive Father God, she presents us with a loving, Mother God. Instead of exalting survival for the few, she declares a democracy of justice and caring. Instead of a dualism of body vs. soul, masculine vs. feminine, human vs. nature, she proclaims unity. Instead of fear, trust. Instead of leading with the reptilian brain, she thinks with the mammal, co-operative brain. Instead of raping and plundering Mother Earth, she honors the divine in nature and the "web of creation" that Hildegard wrote about. Instead of human egoism and narcissism, she issues a new invitation to celebrate and to share. And instead of self-pity and self-aggrandizement, she models a healthy self-love that leads toward service to others.

Julian clearly gifts us with a paradigm shift for religion, from an ideology of original sin to a consciousness of original goodness or original blessing. From guilt to gratitude. From the question that has dominated religion from Julian's day to our own, what the great biblical scholar Krister Stendahl described as the "neurotic question not found in the Bible"—that is, "Am I saved?"—to a question of gratitude and grace: "How do we give thanks and give back to mother earth and the cosmos and all the blessings our species has inherited?"

Rabbi Heschel teaches that a prophet's primary task is to interfere. Julian, by calling us to interfere with patriarchy and heal the wounds that it has wracked upon human history and the human soul and the earth, beckons us from folly to wisdom. Are we listening?

ACKNOWLEDGMENTS

I thank Mirabai Starr for her wise and generous Foreword and for her excellent and lively translation of Julian's book, *Showings*. Also thanks to Brendan Doyle for his excellent and sensitive translation of Julian. Also, my deep thanks to Aaron Stern, founder and president of the Academy for the Love of Learning, for his friendship and encouragement over the years—and also his introducing me to his friend, Gloria Steinem.

I want to thank Dennis Edwards, who keeps the fires burning at our nonprofit on a day-by-day basis as he has done for eighteen years, and Phila Hoopes, Jerry Maynard, Rick Reich, Ellen Kennedy, Ronaldo Tuazon, and the team who keep the *Daily Meditations with Matthew Fox* (dailymeditationswithmatthewfox.org) project alive daily. And to Mary Plaster for her generous work in creating facebook. And all those through the years who have assisted the work of getting creation spirituality into the world by way of publications and course offerings, schools, institutes and universities, with a special shout out to Dr. Mary Ford-Grabowsky, who helped found the University of Creation Spirituality.

I want to thank Ronaldo Tuazon for his enticing cover painting and his friendship. And Jennifer Hereth for her painting on the back cover—she tells me it is an encaustic, an ancient Egyptian method of painting with hot wax.

I wish to thank the many teachers of feminism in my life, including but not limited to the following: Rosemary Ruether, Adrienne Rich, Susan Griffin, M. C. Richards, Joanna Macy, Sister Jose Hobday, Clarissa Pinkola Estes, Sister Dorothy Stang, Suzi Gablik, Hildegard of Bingen, Mechtild of Magdeburg, Riane Eisler, Carol Christ, Starhawk, Louisa Teish, the Sacred Heart Sisters of Barat College, the BVM Sisters of Mundelein College, the Holy Name Sisters of Holy Names College (and Sister Lois MacGillivray, in particular), Meister Eckhart, Thomas Aquinas, Francis of Assisi, Otto Rank, Andrew Harvey, Alessandra Belloni, Lucia Birnbaum, Phyllis Trible, Mary Daly, Marija Gimbutas, Jennifer Berezen, Buck Ghosthorse, Jim Roberts. I salute Jill Angelo for her wise and generous advice and assistance from Christine Colborne at iUniverse who helped bring this book forth.

A special thanks to all of those who have interrupted their very busy schedules to read this book and offer commentary including: Gloria Steinem, Fr. Richard Rohr, OFM, Dr. Clarissa Pinkola Estes, Sr. Joan Chittister, Sr. Simone Campbell, Andrew Harvey, Dr. Rupert Sheldrake, Caroline Myss, Rev. Lauren Artress and Christian de la Huerta.

And, of course, Julian of Norwich who, in accompanying me while writing this book, has taught me, in my eightieth year, what my life has been all about: that to bring alive the creation spirituality tradition again is to bring back the divine feminine and the goddess for women and men alike and how this means standing with indigenous wisdom keepers and also challenging patriarchy. It means to learn wisdom and knowledge and to be both patient and wild, determined and joyful, in the face of a patriarchal backlash that shrinks from relinquishing the privileges that come with reptilian brain dominance.

Last, but not least, I want to thank my sisters, Terry, Roberta, and Tricia, along with my mother Beatrice Fox, for lifelong lessons of what it means to be strong women and independent ones in a world that is often less than friendly to the ways of women.

May Julian give us all vision and courage for the continued journey!

ENDNOTES

Introduction   *Julian's Time of Pandemic and Ours*

1   Edmund Colledge, OSA, and James Walsh, SJ, *A Book of Showings to the Anchoress Julian of Norwich* (Toronto: Pontifical Institute of Mediaeval Studies, 1978), 1:39.

2   Mirabai Starr, *The Showings of Julian of Norwich: A New Translation,* (Charlottesville, VA: Hampton Roads, 2013), xvi.

3   Ibid., xix, xxii.

4   "Thomas Berry," in Mary Ford-Grabowsky, ed., *The Unfolding of a Prophet: Matthew Fox at 60* (Berkeley, CA: self-pub., 2000), 63f.

5   Matthew Fox, *Sheer Joy: Conversations with Thomas Aquinas on Creation Spirituality* (Mineola, NY: Ixia, 2020), 48, 47.

6   Colledge and Walsh, *A Book of Showings*, 1:197.

7   Ibid., 196.

8   Nasrullah Mambrol, "Analysis of T. S. Eliot's Four Quartets," *Literary Theory and Criticism* (July 4, 2020): https://literariness.org/2020/07/04/analysis-of-t-s-eliots-four-quartets/.

9   Thomas Merton, *Cold War Letters* (Maryknoll, NY: Orbis Books, 2006), 104f.

10   See Matthew Fox, *A Way To God: Thomas Merton's Creation Spirituality Journey* (Novato, CA: New World Library, 2016), 143-164.

11   Colledge and Walsh, *Book of Showings,* 1:41, 198.

12   Matthew Fox, *Hildegard of Bingen, a Saint for Our Times: Unleashing Her Power in the 21ˢᵗ Century* (Vancouver: Namaste, 2012), 49.

13   See note 1 above.

14   Starr, *The Showings of Julian of Norwich,* xiv.

15   Ibid., xxii.

16   Brendan Doyle, *Meditations with Julian of Norwich* (Santa Fe, NM: Bear, 1983).

Chapter 1 Facing the Darkness

1 Covering Climate Now, "The Coronavirus Connection," *The Nation* (March 18, 2020): https://www.thenation.com/article/environment/coronavirus-indigenous-peoples/.

2 Cited in Matthew Fox, *Creation Spirituality: Liberating Gifts for the Peoples of the Earth* (San Francisco: HarperSanFrancisco, 1991), 82.

3 I tell the fuller story of Marguerite Porete and her influence on Meister Eckhart in Matthew Fox, *Meister Eckhart: A Mystic-Warrior for Our Times* (Novato, CA: New World Library, 2014), 88–93.

4 Sue Woodruff, *Meditations with Mechtild of Magdeburg* (Santa Fe, NM: Bear, 1982), 60–65.

5 Ibid., 68.

6 Ibid., 69.

7 Ibid., 71.

8 Ibid., 70.

9 John Frederick Nims, *The Poems of St. John of the Cross* (Chicago: University of Chicago Press, 1979), 19, 21.

Chapter 2 Goodness, Joy, Awe

1 Jean Delumeau, *Sin and Fear: The Emergence of a Western Guilt Culture, 13th–18th Centuries*, translated by Eric Nicholson (New York: St. Martin's Press, 1990), 145f.

2 Matthew Fox, *Meditations with Meister Eckhart* (Santa Fe, NM: Bear, 1983), 56.

3 Matthew Fox, ed., *Hildegard of Bingen's Book of Divine Works with Letters and Songs* (Santa Fe, NM: Bear, 1987), 64.

4 Colledge and Walsh, *Book of Showings*, II:463, 752.

5 For more on acedia, see Matthew Fox, *Sins of the Spirit, Blessings of the Flesh: Transforming Evil in Soul and Society* (Berkeley, CA: North Atlantic Books, 2016), 189–236.

6 Abraham Joshua Heschel, *Man Is Not Alone: A Philosophy of Religion* (New York: Farrar, Straus and Young, 1951), 11.

7 Abraham Joshua Heschel, *God in Search of Man: A Philosophy of Judaism* (New York: Farrar, Straus and Cudahy, 1955), 78.

8 Cited in Fox, *Creation Spirituality*, 29.

Chapter 3   The Oneing of God and Nature

1   Woodruff, *Meditations with Mechtild*, 42.
2   Matthew Fox, *Passion for Creation: The Earth-Honoring Spirituality of Meister Eckhart* (Rochester, VT: Inner Traditions, 1991), 512.
3   See Matthew Fox and Bishop Marc Andrus, *Stations of the Cosmic Christ* (Unity Village, MO, Unity Books, 2016).
4   See Matthew Fox, *The Coming of the Cosmic Christ* (San Francisco: HarperSanFrancisco, 1988), 83–128.
5   John O'Donohue *Anam Cara: A Book of Celtic Wisdom* (New York: HarperCollins, 1997), 96f.
6   Fox, *Meditations with Meister Eckhart*, 97.
7   See Fox and Andrus, *Stations of the Cosmic Christ*, 123–28.
8   Thomas Berry, foreword to *Thomas Merton, When the Trees Say Nothing: Writings on Nature*, edited by Kathleen Deignan (Notre Dame, IN: Sorin Books, 2003), 18f.

Chapter 4   The Divine Feminine and Motherhood of God

1   Adrienne Rich, *Of Woman Born: Motherhood as Experience and Institution* (New York: W. W. Norton, 1976), 11f.
2   Ibid., 114f.
3   Woodruff, *Meditations with Mechtild*, 79, 109.
4   Fox, *Hildegard of Bingen*, 114.
5   *Hildegardis Scivias*, edited by Adeloundis Führkötter, OSB, and Angela Carlevaris, OSB (Turnhout: Brepols, 1978), 2:565.
6   See Fox, *Hildegard of Bingen*, 125–32.
7   Ibid., 114f.
8   Ibid., 120.
9   Ibid., xiii.
10   Ibid., 115.
11   Fox, *Passion for Creation*, 291.
12   See Fox, *Meister Eckhart*, 66f.
13   Matthew Fox, *The Tao of Thomas Aquinas: Fierce Wisdom for Hard Times* (Bloomington, IN: iUniverse, 2020), 115.
14   See Matthew Fox, "On Desentimentalizing Spirituality," in Matthew Fox, *Wrestling with the Prophets: Creation Spirituality in Everyday Life* (New York: Jeremy Tarcher, 2003), 297–316.
15   John Dominic Crossan, *In Search of Paul: How Jesus's Apostle Opposed Rome's Empire with God's Kingdom* (San Francisco: HarperSanFrancisco, 2004), 278–91.

16 See Matthew Fox, *Illuminations of Hildegard of Bingen* (Rochester, VT: Bear, 2002), 76–82 and plate 9.

Chapter 5   Tasting Non-dualism

1 William Hermanns, *Einstein and the Poet: In Search of the Cosmic Man* (Brookline Village, MA: Branden, 1983), 68f.
2 See "Sermon 3" in Matthew Fox, *Passion for Creation,* 77.
3 Ibid., 312.
4 Ibid., 302.
5 Fox, *Sheer Joy,* 89.
6 Ibid., 167.
7 Ibid., 168.
8 Ibid.
9 Fox, *Meditations with Meister Eckhart,* 58.

Chapter 6   Trusting Our Sensuality

1 William Eckhardt, *Compassion: Toward a Science of Value* (Oakville, Ontario: CPRI, 1973), 4f.
2 Gerhard von Rad, *Wisdom in Israel* (Nashville: Abingdon, 1974), 306.
3 Roland E. Murphy, "Wisdom Theses," in *Wisdom and Knowledge*, (n.d.), 2:190.
4 Walter Brueggemann, "The Trusted Creature," *Catholic Biblical Quarterly*, 31 (1969): 486f., 489.
5 Ibid., 492, 491, 495. I take up the theme of *trust* as one of the basic principles of creation spirituality in Matthew Fox, *Original Blessing: A Primer in Creation Spirituality* (New York: Jeremy P. Tarcher/Putnam, 2000), 81–87.
6 Fox, *Tao of Thomas Aquinas,* 155.
7 Fox, *Meditations with Meister Eckhart,* 82.
8 Fox, *Sheer Joy,* 149f.
9 Ibid., 146–52.
10 Fox, *Hildegard of Bingen,* 34.
11 Woodruff, *Meditations with Mechtild,* 43.
12 Ibid., 41.
13 Ibid.
14 Ibid., 39.
15 For the entire poem and an exegesis of it see Fox, *The Coming of the Cosmic Christ,* 112–14.
16 Rich, *Of Woman Born,* 284–86.
17 Wendell Berry, *The Unsettling of America: Culture and Agriculture* (San Francisco: Avon Books, 1977), 107f.

18   Ibid., 123f.

19   Fox, *Passion for Creation*, 72.

Chapter 7   *The Power of Love Over Evil: A Call to Wellness*

1   Fox, *Sheer Joy*, 229.

2   "Papal Bulls that Create the Foundation of the Doctrine of Discovery," *Doctrine of Discovery: Mother Earth's Pandemic*: https://doctrineofdiscovery. org/papal-bulls/.

3   Andrew Harvey and Carolyn Baker, *Radical Regeneration: Birthing the New Human in the Age of Extinction* (Bloomington, IN: iUniverse, forthcoming).

4   Ibid.

5   Ibid.

6   Ibid.

7   Fox, *Tao of Thomas Aquinas*, 154.

Conclusion   *Why Julian? Why Now?*

1   Fox, *Sheer Joy*, 89, 93, 59.

2   Ibid., 101.

3   "Papal Bull Dum Diversas 18 June 1452," *Doctrine of Discovery: Mother Earth's Pandemic*: https://doctrineofdiscovery.org/dum-diversas/.

4   "The Legal Battle and Spiritual War against the Native People: The Bull Inter Caetera (Alexander VI) May 4, 1493," *Doctrine of Discovery: Mother Earth's Pandemic*: https://doctrineofdiscovery.org/inter-caetera/.

5   "Discovery doctrine," *Wikipedia*, accessed August 22, 2020: https://en.wikipedia. org/wiki/Discovery_doctrine.

6   Robert Bellah, *The Broken Covenant: American Civil Religion in Time of Trial* (New York: Seabury, 1975), 162.

Epilogue   *A Prophet for the Twenty-First Century*

1   Marija Gimbutas, *The Language of the Goddess* (San Francisco: HarperSanFrancisco, 1989), 321.

ABOUT THE AUTHOR

Matthew Fox is author of thirty-eight books on culture and spirituality, which have been translated into seventy-seven languages and received many awards. He graduated from the Institut catholique de Paris with a doctorate in the history and theology of spiritualities. In his books and teaching and designing of spirituality programs, he has brought alive the much neglected western tradition of creation spirituality.

He lectures internationally and has created a pedagogy for teaching spirituality that has reached many thousands of persons through Mundelein College in Chicago, Holy Names College, and the University of Creation Spirituality, which he founded and led for nine years in Oakland, California, along with his pilot program, YELLAWE, for inner city youth.

For speaking out on women's right, gay rights, and Native American rights, he was silenced for a year and later expelled from the Dominican Order under the papacies of John Paul II and Benedict XVI. He then joined the Episcopal Church to work with young people to create a postmodern form of ritual and worship known as the "Cosmic Mass" that incorporates dance, DJ, VJ, rap, and other postmodern art forms. He is cofounder of the Order of the Sacred Earth and, since Mother's Day 2019, has offered free daily meditations at dailymeditationswithmatthewfox.org.

Fox is a visiting scholar at the Academy for the Love of Learning in Santa Fe, New Mexico, and teaches frequently on the Shift Network. He is a recipient of the Abbey Courage of Conscience Peace Award, whose other recipients include the Dalai Lama, Rosa Parks, Mother Teresa, Ernesto Cardinale, and Maya Angelou. Other awards include the Gandhi, King, Ikeda Community Builder Prize from Morehouse College, the Humanities Award of the Sufi International Association of Sufism, the Tikkun Ethics

Award, INTA Humanitarian Award, and the New Thought Walden Award. See www.matthewfox.org.

About his work, the late Father Bede Griffiths said: Matthew Fox's "creation spirituality is the spirituality of the future and his theology of the Cosmic Christ is the theology of the future." Father Thomas Berry said: "Matthew Fox might well be the most creative, the most comprehensive, surely the most challenging religious-spiritual thinker that has emerged from within the contemporary Christian tradition in America. He has the scholarship, the imagination, the courage, the writing skill to fulfill this role at a time when the more official Christian theological traditions are having difficulty in establishing any vital contact with either the spiritual possibilities of the present or with their own most creative spiritual traditions of the past."

Mirabai Starr (foreword) has received critical acclaim for her contemporary translations of Julian of Norwich as well as St. John of the Cross and Teresa of Ávila. Her most recent book is *Wild Mercy: Living the Fierce and Tender Wisdom of the Women Mystics* (Sounds True, 2019).

Permission pending from University of Chicago Press for Frederick Nims translation of "Dark Night" poem by John of the Cross

BOOKS BY MATTHEW FOX

Original Blessing

The Coming of the Cosmic Christ

A Spirituality Named Compassion

Order of the Sacred Earth: An Intergenerational Vision of Love and Action (with Skylar Wilson and Jennifer Listug)

Prayer: A Radical Response to Life

Creation Spirituality: Liberating Gifts for the Peoples of the Earth

Whee! We, Wee All the Way Home: Toward a Prophetic, Sensual Spirituality

Western Spirituality: Historical Roots, Ecumenical Routes (editor)

Natural Grace (with Rupert Sheldrake)

The Physics of Angels (with Rupert Sheldrake)

Christian Mystics: 365 Readings and Meditations

Passion for Creation: Meister Eckhart's Earth-Honoring Spirituality

Meister Eckhart: A Mystic-Warrior for Our Times

Meditations with Meister Eckhart

Illuminations of Hildegard of Bingen

Hildegard of Bingen, A Saint for Our Times: Unleashing Her Power in the 21ˢᵗ Century

Hildegard of Bingen's Book of Divine Works, Songs and Letters

Sheer Joy: Conversations with Thomas Aquinas on Creation Spirituality

A Way to God: Thomas Merton's Creation Spirituality Journey

The Reinvention of Work: A New Vision of Livelihood for Our Times

Creativity: Where the Divine and the Human Meet

The Hidden Spirituality of Men: Ten Metaphors to Awaken the Sacred Masculine

The A.W.E Project: Reinventing Education, Reinventing the Human

Occupy Spirituality: A Radical Vision for a New Generation (with Adam Bucko)

Sins of the Spirit, Blessings of the Flesh: Transforming Evil in Soul and Society

Wrestling with the Prophets: Essays on Creations Spirituality and Everyday Life

The Pope's War: Why Ratzinger's Secret Crusade Has Imperiled the Church and What Can Be Saved

Confessions: The Making of a Post-Denominational Priest

One River, Many Wells: Wisdom Springing from Global Faiths

Religion USA: Culture and Religion by way of Time *Magazine*

A New Reformation

Letters to Pope Francis

Naming the Unnameable: 89 Wonderful and Useful Names for God . . . Including the Unnameable God

Stations of the Cosmic Christ (with Bishop Marc Andrus)

The Lotus & the Rose: Dialogs on Buddhism and Christian Mysticism (with Lama Tsomo)

The Tao of Thomas Aquinas: Fierce Wisdom for Hard Times

To order any of these books, visit matthewfox.org.

The Tao of Thomas Aquinas: Fierce Wisdom for Hard Times
By Matthew Fox

A stunning Spiritual Handbook drawn from the substantive teachings of a mystical/prophetic genius offering a sublime roadmap for spirituality and action, this short book brings a well of deep wisdom to the surface.

Publisher : iUniverse (January 31, 2020)   Paperback : 280 pages
ISBN-10 : 1532093411   ISBN-13 : 978-1532093418
Available at booksellers in paperback, e-book,
and audiobook (digital and cd set)
www.matthewfox.org

Praise for *The Tao of Thomas Aquinas:*
Fierce Wisdom for Hard Times

What a wonderful book! The Tao of Thomas Aquinas is a masterpiece. --Caroline Myss

Who knew that Thomas Aquinas was so extravagantly blessing the holiness of all that is incarnational while exalting the One that transcends all distinction? --Mirabai Starr

This is a beautiful book, a book written in a way that brings this great medieval theologian's mystical vision into a living reality. --From the Forward by Ilia Delio

Whatever path you are on, read this book and be renewed by its illumined passion for the titanic work ahead. –Andrew Harvey

Matthew breaks new ground in appreciating the great saint's spiritual depths and practical wisdom. This handbook offers a guide for all to stand up, be counted and make a difference. –Rev. Richard Rohr, OFM

Sheer Joy: Conversations with Thomas
Aquinas on Creation Spirituality
By Matthew Fox

Renowned theologian Matthew Fox "interviews" Thomas Aquinas
in a provocative reevaluation of the spirituality of the 13th-century
saint. Fox reveals a passionate, prophetic, and mystical celebrator
of the blessings of creation. The author speaks with Aquinas in
a modern forum, questioning the saint about the Four Paths of
creation spirituality; the responses are culled from Aquinas's works
that include many passages never before translated into English.

Publisher : Ixia Press   Paperback : 560 pages
ISBN-10 : 0486842010   ISBN-13 : 978-0486842011
Available at booksellers. www.matthewfox.org

Daily Meditations with Matthew Fox
www.DailyMeditationsWithMatthewFox.Org

Calling all Lovers of Creation, Social and Environmental Activists, Mystic Explorers, Sacred Earth Keepers:

On Mother's Day, May 12, 2019, in honor of Gaia, our wounded Mother Earth, I and a dedicated team of helpers, launched a series of daily meditations to support your being and your work. We launched a Free Daily Meditation that will support your inner and outer work, your contemplation and your action, your mystical and prophetic vocations.

Some of the meditations are brand new and some are drawn from my past writings. I hope you will join me in this daily meditation project and invite your friends and families and communities to join as well.

In these meditations I draw out themes that I have been developing in my work for the last fifty years where I tried to take treasures from the burning building of our Western spiritual heritage to inspire and train mystics and prophets. We are creating a conversation with emerging movements of eco and gender justice as well as those of interfaith or deep ecumenism. My goal is to create a creation-centered vision and practice for a spirituality that can nurture and help sustain mystics and prophets for our times with a "Great Turning" upon us. Creation spirituality has always been eager to incorporate science and in our day a new cosmology assists us to grow our souls larger and our hearts stronger. Hopefully by drawing on the riches of the Creation Spirituality lineage we can be better empowered to carry on healthy resistance and inspire creativity that leads to authentic transformation of hearts as well as structures.

Matthew Fox

CPSIA information can be obtained
at www.ICGtesting.com
Printed in the USA
BVHW080304200821
614531BV00003B/304